A Rational Portal to Infinity

A New Era handbook to discover your Infinite Self

Praveen Dixit

Let our story evolve in the light of awakened consciousness. See through the clouds of beliefs and narratives. **You are infinite.**

Contents

Preface 5

Introduction 7

PART 1 – LIMITED TRUTHS 10

The Experience of Body 11

The Story of I Am 23

Me and The World 32

Limiting Happiness 40

PART 2 – THE GRAND DISCOVERY 48

The Path of Science 49

The Path of Religion 61

The Independent Truth 70

Side Effects: Peace and Fearlessness 82

PART 3- EVOLUTION IN AWAKENED CONSCIOUSNESS 92

The Gradual Alignment 93

Appearance Continues 104

Intelligence in Awakened Space 114

Formal and Informal Practices 127

For more information or to get in touch

Visit

OneInsight.in

Preface

I feel a sense of relief having gathered and arranged my thoughts on Spiritual Awakening and the discovery of Infinity for our current, rational, and relatively mature society. A society mature enough to understand that spirituality is not just a distant topic for a select few nearing the end of their life journey.

The ego or ignorance, like a stack of hay, was dry enough here for various reasons, worldly or otherwise. A few sparks were enough to set it ablaze, revealing the space of presence.

I never intended to share this with anyone verbally, let alone write a book about Self-realisation, the 'Self' with a capital 'S'. The journey, unplanned at the start, was personal, like most of us. However, I soon realized that defining my identity by my past story was not only incomplete but fundamentally flawed. I knew there were things I was certain of when I let go of the mental narrative of who or what is here. What began as a fleeting glimpse into my non-egoic identity gradually permeated my waking state.

My journey to understand the mystery of being human began as a mental quest in 2012. There were reliable sources and sages discussing these matters of inner work. Being the skeptic and atheist I was then, I was careful not to become desperate and fall into blind followership. Looking back, I see this was key in authentically discovering and living the profound wisdoms and insights of spiritual traditions.

While I was in the process of understanding the concept of Non-Duality mentally, practicing awareness exercises, meditations, and contemplations were translating it into an experiential reality. My only desire was to know who I truly am, beyond my story or the narrative given by human society, written or verbal. I spent about a year and a half in the lower Himalayas of Himachal Pradesh, making friends and discussing the practicality of spirituality in today's world. I also learned about their perspectives and struggles in life. At the heart of every suffering was the overlooked pristine sense of self within.

When I first considered writing this book in 2019, I was determined not to discuss these matters unless they were a living reality for me. This is a subject where many thinkers and half-baked gurus are already creating a distorted, even damaging, image of what awakening is. They are mostly causing more division in society and have excluded the scientific momentum that has shaped the current world's mental narrative. Therefore, I have made it a point to be inclusive while also relentlessly pointing out the limitations of dualistic investigations of Science and the Dogmas of Religion. I share this writing in the hope of guiding you on the path of non-belief, the non-conceptual Truth, if you haven't found it yet.

I envision of a society built on the value of non-separation that is inherently natural, and I am ready to do whatever I can to serve this cause. 'A Rational Portal to Infinity' is a step towards that goal. It starts at the individual level. Our happiness, clarity of who we are, and our relationship with the world matter. The clarity that comes from self-discovery guides you not only in times of joy but also in times of chaos.

Introduction

The Infinity, as we refer to it, is the origin of all physical, emotional and mental experiences. This Source can be labelled in various ways – God, the ultimate scientific discovery, the unknowable mystery, and so on. It encompasses the source of the body-mind complex, the medium through which we live and interpret our experiences.

Our pursuit of peripheral happiness and fulfilment is, in essence, an attempt to discover this ultimate Source which can be labelled as Infinity. There exists a simpler, more direct, and rational approach to living from this space – an approach that is fearless and playful. With time, you will come to realize that you are not separate from this Source. In fact, you are already within the Source of everything. This realization is a transformative journey towards self-discovery and unity with the universe.

In this book, you will uncover the innate, unconditional happiness that has been obscured by the process of adapting to external circumstances. You will delve into the aware space within, poised to respond gracefully without losing sight of your pristine identity. This direct perception does not require you to subscribe to another narrative of creation. Instead, we employ the classical method of "Self-enquiry," complemented by relevant and specific meditation and mindfulness exercises which is in the end of this book.

The insights gained during the reading will not contradict the existing scientific paradigm. Far from alienating you from existing art, technology, or the essence of religious teachings, this book will enable you to approach these aspects with greater clarity and involvement than ever before. The goal is to align your internal voice with the Source or Your Infinite Self, enhancing your understanding and appreciation of the world around you.

Awakening is not a singular event, but rather a continuous journey that necessitates the right motivation and a sense of curiosity. With this understanding, the book is structured into three parts to guide the readers through potent contemplations and practical awareness exercises in the end. The book and suggested Formal and Informal practices can be utilized regularly until one reaches the pristine space within themselves. Remember, the path to awakening is not a sprint, but a marathon, requiring consistent effort and exploration.

Important Note:

If you are already on the path of Spiritual Awakening, you can directly skip to the last section of Formal and Informal Practices. You can choose to read the chapters that interest you for the love of reading. For readers who are new or have spent time selectively in this exploration, this is an opportunity to make a quantum shift in the evolution of your soul into a more divine realm and profoundly fulfilling life on Earth.

The highest teaching in spirituality is Silence. That said, we are at a point in human evolution where our ignorance is a result of conditioning by language. Henceforth, I am using another thorn to remove the one we have right now. Pardon me for using words to point you to that which is beyond the scope of language.

Words and sentences are an arrangement of symbols in a prescribed order, which constitutes the rules of a language. The conceptual understanding, at best, can serve as a pointer to see the highest within you when in a spiritual context. However, making meaning and imagination can never reflect the absolute truth. Please translate the sentences you read to experience with all your body and the environment you are in, whenever you contemplate. Remembering or trying to understand sentences alone will not lead to an insight.

Part 1 – Limited Truths

Chapter 1

The Experience of Body

"Silence is a source of great strength." - Lao Tzu

The non-dual approach to spirituality is a profound perspective that transcends the conventional dichotomy of self and other, mind and body, and the temporal and eternal. It posits that all phenomena, including the human body, are manifestations of a single, unified reality. The human body is not seen as separate from the divine, but rather as a unique expression of it. Every cell, every organ, every breath is a manifestation of the same underlying reality that pervades the entire universe. This view challenges the common perception of the body as a mere physical entity, separate and distinct from the spiritual realm. Instead, it invites us to recognize the body as a sacred vessel, imbued with divine presence.

This book embraces an inclusive approach. At times, the journey of self-discovery might heavily favor the denial of the physical world's reality, perceiving it as an illusion. However, this viewpoint is not adopted here, as it's difficult to disregard our bodily experiences and the world that surrounds us. The renowned non-dualistic phrase 'Brahma-Satyam Jagat-Mithyā Jivo Brahmaiva Nāparaḥ' translates to English as follows:

Brahman, an intelligence that is both formless and capable of taking form, is the only reality. 'Jagat-Mithyā' can be loosely translated as the world being an illusion or false. However, 'Mithya', or illusion, holds true only when we perceive the phenomenal world from an ego-centric perspective. Reality is a unified whole, and we, as human beings and the world, are nothing but manifestations of that non conceptual Brahman.

As we journey towards recognizing ourselves as observers of our bodies, mental narratives, and the world, it's crucial to continually scrutinize the nature of the things we know and conclusions made about them. The ultimate unification of the observer and the observed, seen as different expressions of the One, constitutes a holistic path.

This brings a new dimension to spiritual practice: embodied spirituality. Rather than seeking transcendence of the physical body, embodied spirituality encourages us to fully inhabit our bodies and to experience the divine through our physical senses. It teaches us that spiritual awakening is not an escape from the body, but a deeper engagement with it. Through practices of meditation, and mindful movement, we can cultivate a more intimate relationship with our bodies and discover the sacred within the ordinary. By recognizing the body as a manifestation of the divine, we can approach illness and healing from a holistic perspective. Rather than seeing illness as a malfunction of the body, we can view it as a call to bring our lives back into alignment with the underlying wholeness of reality. Healing, in this context, is not just about curing symptoms, but about reconnecting with our inherent wholeness and the divine presence within us.

The physical being as a medium of experience

The human body offers a transformative perspective that can deepen our understanding of the nature of consciousness, and awaken us to the sacredness of our physical existence. By recognizing the body as a manifestation of the divine, we can move beyond the illusion of separation and experience the profound interconnectedness of all life. In the words of the mystic poet Rumi, "You are not a drop in the ocean. You are the entire ocean in a drop." The human body is more than just a physical entity; it is an instrument that allows us to experience the world around us and consequentially be the ocean itself. From the perspective of mindfulness and awakened consciousness, the body serves as a gateway to evolve spiritually and connection with our surroundings.

Every sensation we feel, every movement we make, is a testament to the body's role as an instrument of awareness to experience and express. Our senses - sight, hearing, touch, taste, and smell - provide us with a constant stream of information about the world around us. These sensory experiences, when observed mindfully, can bring us into a state of heightened awareness and presence that is our natural state of being.

Mindfulness, the practice of bringing one's attention to experiences occurring in the present moment, invites us to tune into our bodies. It encourages us to observe our sensations without judgment, to fully experience the richness of the present moment. This mindful attention to the body anchors us in the here and now, allowing us to engage more fully with our experiences.

Awakened consciousness, often described as a state of heightened awareness and connection with one's true self, is deeply intertwined with our physical bodies. The body is not just a vessel for this awakened consciousness; it is an active participant in its unfolding. Through mindful movement and relaxed attention, we can quiet the unconscious and conscious mental noise and open the door to deeper levels of consciousness. The body, in its wisdom, guides us along this path, offering insights and experiences that are inaccessible to the intellectual mind alone. It allows us to experience the world in its fullness, to connect with the present moment. By honoring and attending to our bodies, we can enrich our experiences and navigate the world with greater awareness and presence.

Symphony of sensations

The human body is a remarkable instrument of perception, constantly experiencing a myriad of sensations. From the gentle caress of a breeze to the rhythmic beating of our hearts, our bodies are continuously sensing and interacting with the world around us.

Our bodies are equipped with an intricate network of sensory receptors that allow us to experience the world. These receptors detect a wide range of stimuli, including temperature, pressure, pain, and body position. Every moment, our bodies are flooded with sensory information, creating a continuous stream of sensations. These sensations are not just passive experiences; they play an active role in how we navigate and interact with the world. They inform us about our environment, guide our movements, and even shape our perceptions and beliefs.

Mindfulness practices offer a powerful way to tune into our body's sensations. By bringing a non-judgmental awareness to our sensory experiences, we can cultivate a deeper connection with our bodies. This mindful body awareness can reveal a wealth of insights. We may notice subtle sensations that we typically overlook, such as the feeling of our feet touching the ground or the sensation of breath entering and leaving our bodies. We may also become more aware of how our bodies respond to different situations, helping us to better understand and manage our reactions.

Our bodies and emotions are deeply interconnected. Emotions are often experienced as physical sensations in the body. For example, anxiety might be felt as a tightening in the chest, while joy might be experienced as a warmth spreading through the body, peace is felt as muscles relaxing in the neck region. By recognizing our body as a bundle of sensations, we can become more attuned to our emotional states. This can enhance our emotional intelligence, improve our mental health, and enrich our overall quality of life. Understanding our body as a bundle of sensations opens up a new way of experiencing ourselves and the world. It invites us to engage more fully with our sensory experiences, to cultivate

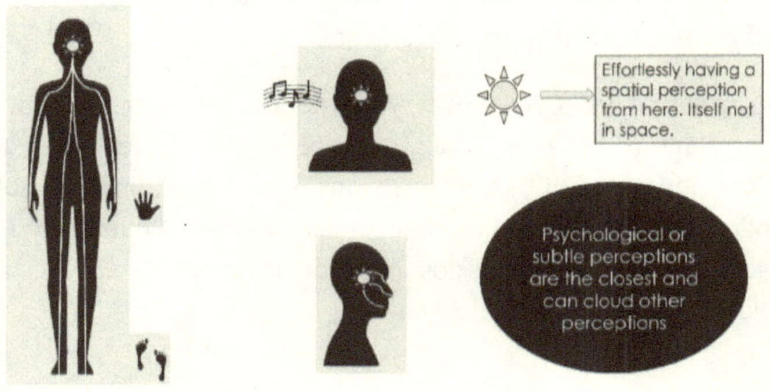

mindfulness and body awareness, and to explore the intricate interplay between our bodies and our emotions.

The above image highlights that Knowing yourself (Intuitively) as the ground zero of all the sensory perceptions and the subtle perception is the key. Naturally you will see that your attention will rest in the point of knowing marked by Sun.

Brain and Consciousness

The subjective experience of an individual's inner life, is one of the most fascinating and elusive topics in neuroscience and philosophy. Despite significant advancements in brain research, understanding consciousness remains a formidable challenge. We will explore the limitations of understanding consciousness through the brain and delves into the 'hard problem' of consciousness. Modern neuroscience has made remarkable strides in mapping the brain and identifying correlations between brain activity and conscious experiences. Techniques such as functional Magnetic Resonance Imaging (fMRI) and Electroencephalography (EEG) have provided insights into the brain regions associated with various cognitive functions and states of consciousness.

However, understanding consciousness solely through the lens of brain activity presents several limitations:

Correlation vs. Causation: While neuroscience can identify correlations between brain activity (Neural Correlates of Consciousness, NCC) and conscious experiences, it does not necessarily imply causation. It remains unclear whether brain activity produces consciousness or if they merely occur simultaneously.

Subjectivity: Consciousness is inherently subjective, experienced uniquely by each individual. This subjectivity is challenging to study objectively using brain imaging techniques, which provide only an external view of brain activity.

Neural Complexity: The brain is extraordinarily complex, with approximately 86 billion neurons interconnected in intricate networks. The complexity of these networks and their interactions makes it difficult to pinpoint how consciousness arises from brain activity.

The 'hard problem' of consciousness, a term coined by philosopher David Chalmers, refers to the question of how and why physical processes in the brain give rise to the subjective experience of consciousness. While the 'easy problems' of consciousness concern the mechanisms of perception, cognition, and motor control, the 'hard problem' grapples with why these processes should be accompanied by conscious experience at all.

The hard problem poses a significant challenge to neuroscience for several reasons:

Qualia: Qualia refer to the subjective experiences of consciousness, such as the redness of red or the pain of a headache. These experiences are subjective and personal, making them difficult to measure or examine through objective scientific methods. While one may measure the electrical activity and observe the pattern for the experience, we experience a quality of the phenomenal event and not the experience of electric shocks in the brain.

The Explanatory Gap: There is an explanatory gap between the physical processes in the brain and the subjective experiences of consciousness. Despite understanding the mechanisms of perception, we lack a comprehensive explanation of how and why these processes result in conscious experience.

The Binding Problem: The binding problem refers to the question of how the brain integrates information from various sources into a unified conscious experience. Despite extensive research, this remains a largely unresolved issue.

While neuroscience has provided valuable insights into the correlations between brain activity and conscious experience, it faces significant challenges in explaining the subjective nature of consciousness. The hard problem of consciousness highlights these limitations, emphasizing the gap between physical processes and subjective experiences. As we continue to explore the enigma of consciousness, it is crucial to acknowledge these challenges and seek a multidisciplinary approach, incorporating insights from neuroscience, philosophy, psychology, and potentially other fields yet unknown.

Reasonable misconception of being merely the physical self

Allow me to articulate the perspective of spiritual visionaries who staunchly uphold the conviction that they are not their bodies. The path of spiritual enlightenment often leads to a profound revelation: we are more than just our physical forms. This section delves into the valid misperception of identifying oneself as merely the body and its spiritual implications. The notion "I am this body" is a fundamental illusion that permeates our daily consciousness. From birth, we are conditioned to associate our identity with our physical form, perceiving ourselves as isolated beings, confined within our bodily boundaries, separate from the world around us.

This identification with the body is reinforced by our sensory experiences. We navigate the world through our senses, which are intrinsically linked to our physical form. Our experiences of touch, sight, taste, smell, and hearing all affirm the reality of our physical existence. In contrast, many spiritual traditions propose a different perspective. They suggest that our true nature transcends our physical form. In these traditions, the body is seen as a temporary vessel, a vehicle for the soul or consciousness to experience the physical world. The spiritual journey often involves a shift in identity from the body to something more expansive. This could be described as the soul, the Self, consciousness, or simply awareness. This shift is often accompanied by a sense of liberation, a freedom from the limitations imposed by identification with the physical form.

The identification with the body is closely tied to the ego, the sense of "I" or "me". The ego defines itself in relation to the physical form. It says, "I am this body. I am young or old, healthy or sick, attractive or unattractive." These identifications form the basis of the ego's sense of self. However, the ego-self is inherently unstable. It is subject to change and decay, just like the physical body. This leads to a constant struggle to maintain and protect the identity of "I am this body", often resulting in suffering. The realization "I am not this body" is a significant milestone in the spiritual journey. It represents a shift from the ego-self to a more expansive sense of identity. This realization often arises through practices such as meditation, self-inquiry, or mindfulness, which cultivate a direct experience of consciousness. When we recognize that we are not merely our bodies, we open ourselves to a deeper dimension of being. We begin to experience ourselves as awareness, as presence, as the witnessing consciousness that is aware of the body but not limited to it. The mistaken identity of "I am this body" is a fundamental illusion that shapes our experience of ourselves and the world. By recognizing this illusion, we can begin to transcend the limitations of the physical form and awaken to our true nature. This shift in identity is not a denial of the body, but rather a recognition of the deeper reality that underlies sensations and at the same time transcends the physical form.

Happiness arises from realizing we are consciousness

Happiness is a universal pursuit, a feeling that everyone strives to experience. However, the source of true happiness often eludes us, buried beneath layers of misconceptions and misguided pursuits. This part highlights the profound happiness that arises within the body when we gain existential clarity and recognize our true nature as consciousness.

In our quest for happiness, we often seek external sources of joy, which is absolutely fine as long as we do not solely depend on the select activities alone for fulfilment. Whether we admit it or not, often masked by narratives, we chase after material possessions, social validation, and sensory pleasures, believing that they will bring us lasting happiness. However, these external sources of happiness are transient and subject to change, leaving us in a constant state of wanting and planning the next activity.

Existential clarity refers to the profound understanding of our true nature. It is the realization that we are not merely our thoughts, emotions, or physical bodies, but the consciousness that underlies all these experiences. This consciousness is unchanging, limitless, and inherently peaceful. When we recognize this truth, we experience a deep sense of peace and happiness that is independent of external circumstances. While we are not merely our bodies, our bodies play a crucial role in experiencing this existential happiness.

The body is the vessel through which consciousness experiences the world. When we gain existential clarity, this understanding permeates our entire being, including our physical bodies. This existential happiness is not a fleeting emotion but a steady state of being that is felt throughout the body. It may manifest as a sense of lightness, a feeling of expansive warmth, or a profound sense of peace and well-being. These sensations are not dependent on external stimuli but arise from the deep recognition of our true nature.

Cultivating mindfulness and body awareness can help us tune into these subtle sensations of existential happiness, happy to be alive. By bringing a gentle, non-judgmental attention to our bodily sensations, we can become more attuned to the happiness that arises from existential clarity. Mindfulness practices, such as meditation and non-dual contemplations, can be particularly helpful in cultivating this body awareness. These practices invite us to slow down, turn inward, and pay attention to our moment-to-moment experiences. As we cultivate this awareness, we become more receptive to the subtle sensations of existential happiness. The happiness that arises from existential clarity is a profound, sustainable, embodied experience that transcends our usual understanding of happiness. It is not dependent on external circumstances but arises from the deep recognition of our true nature as consciousness.

Chapter 2

The Story of I Am

"The menu is not the meal." - Alan Watts

The concept of identity is often confined to the realm of "I am something" - a statement that ties us to a particular role, profession, or characteristic. However, our existence transcends these labels. We are, first and foremost, a presence, an awareness that exists before any labels are applied. We will explore the fact that we are more than our mental conclusions and how these conclusions can limit our identity.

Before we identify ourselves as a person with a specific role or characteristic, we exist as a presence, a consciousness. This presence is the fundamental essence of our being, existing before any labels or identities are formed. It is the pure "I am" before the "I am something". This presence is not confined by time, space, or any physical attributes. It is the silent observer, the constant in the ever-changing flow of life. Recognizing this presence allows us to see beyond the limitations of our perceived identity and connect with the limitless potential of our true nature. Our mental conclusions about who we are can often limit our identity. These conclusions are formed based on our experiences, societal norms, and expectations. They create a box of "I am this" or "I am that", confining our identity to specific roles or characteristics.

These mental conclusions can limit our growth and potential. They create boundaries that prevent us from exploring aspects of ourselves that do not fit into these predefined categories. Moreover, they can lead to a disconnect from our true nature, causing feelings of dissatisfaction and unrest. Breaking free from these limitations involves recognizing that we are more than our mental conclusions. It involves connecting with the presence that exists before the person, the pure “I am”. This recognition can be facilitated through practices such as meditation, mindfulness, and self-inquiry.

Profession

Our professional identity, the way we perceive ourselves in our profession, often becomes an integral part of our overall self-concept. This identity, shaped by education, work environment, and personal experiences, can provide a sense of belonging, increase job satisfaction, and promote career development. However, a strong identification with a profession can also lead to increased stress, especially when professional demands conflict with personal life, leading to a struggle to maintain work-life balance. High expectations and pressure to perform can result in chronic stress, potentially leading to burnout.

Moreover, individuals with a strong professional identity may find it challenging to detach from work during their leisure time, leading to a constant state of stress. This inability to 'switch off' can have detrimental effects on both physical and mental health.

Spiritual well-being, a sense of peace and purpose in life, can be influenced by various factors, including stress levels. High levels of stress associated with a strong professional identity can dampen spiritual well-being. When one's identity is strongly tied to their profession, they may neglect other aspects of their life, including their spiritual needs. This neglect can lead to a feeling of emptiness or lack of fulfilment, also known as midlife crisis. Moreover, constant stress can make it difficult for individuals to engage in spiritual practices, which require peace of mind.

Ensuring that professional demands do not overshadow personal needs and spiritual well-being is crucial. Employers can play a role in this by promoting a healthy work environment that values work-life balance. Individuals can also take steps to manage stress and nurture their spiritual well-being, such as setting boundaries between work and personal life, engaging in stress-relieving activities, and making time for spiritual practices. Recognizing that our professions are a significant part of our lives, but they do not completely define us, can help mitigate stress and enhance our spiritual well-being.

Relationships

Identity when limited by ego is a complex construct that is influenced by various factors, including our relationships. A strong identification with our relationships can shape our self-perception and influence our experiences. However, this strong identity can also lead to disappointments and hinder the process of spiritual awakening. Relationship identity refers to the part of our self-concept that is derived from our roles in relationships, such as being a parent, spouse, friend, or colleague. A strong relationship identity can provide a sense of belonging and purpose. However, it can also lead to high expectations and dependency on others for validation and happiness.

When our happiness and self-worth are tied to our relationships, disappointments can have a significant impact. If a relationship does not meet our expectations or ends, it can lead to feelings of failure, rejection, and low self-esteem. This can result in emotional distress and can affect our overall well-being. Spiritual awakening is a process of becoming aware of our true nature beyond our physical existence and ego-driven identities. It involves recognizing that we are more than our roles and responsibilities and connecting with our inner self or consciousness. This doesn't imply neglecting the needs and desires of those you care about. Rather, it's about setting aside some time for yourself to explore and understand the deeper truths of human existence.

A strong relationship identity can slow down the awakening process. It's crucial to distinguish between a relationship rooted in love and one that's characterized as strong relationship identity. A relationship based on love tends to result in more thoughtful and considerate outcomes, while a strong relationship can often lead to feelings of anger and resistance, and can be filled with expectations and disappointments. When we become deeply engrossed in our relationships, our focus tends to shift externally, concentrating on others and our roles concerning them. This external focus can divert us from introspection and acknowledging our authentic selves. Furthermore, the emotional upheaval resulting from relationship disappointments can pose additional obstacles to the process of spiritual awakening. It can generate mental disturbances and unrest, making it challenging to attain the tranquility and lucidity necessary for spiritual enlightenment. This act is not one of selfishness; indeed, the peace within you will be mirrored in your relationships.

Moving beyond relationship identity involves recognizing that we are more than our roles in relationships. It involves shifting our focus from external validation including in social media to internal validation, from seeking happiness in others to finding happiness within ourselves. This does not mean abandoning our relationships but rather changing the way we perceive and engage in them. It involves engaging in relationships out of love and genuine connection rather than need and dependency. Practices such as mindfulness, meditation, and self-inquiry can facilitate this shift. They can help us become more aware of our thoughts and emotions, recognize our patterns, and connect with our inner self.

Emotions

Emotions have a big part in our lives, but we often aren't fully aware of our emotional states. They guide our choices, shape how we interact with others, and affect our experience of the sensory perceptions every moment. When we start to identify with our emotions as who we are, it can lead to more highs and lows in life and make it harder to see the spiritual truth. 'Emotion identity' is how much we see our emotions as part of ourselves. When we have a strong emotion identity, we see our emotions as a key part of who we are. We might describe ourselves based on our emotions, like saying "I'm someone who gets angry easily" or "I'm someone who is usually happy".

Emotions are transient by nature - they come and go, rise and fall. When we identify strongly with our emotions, we ride these waves, experiencing intense highs when we feel positive emotions and deep lows when we feel negative emotions. This emotional roller coaster can lead to instability and distress. It can make us reactive, causing us to make impulsive decisions based on our current emotional state. It can also affect our relationships, as we may project our emotions onto others.

A strong emotion identity can also lead to a loss of objective spiritual truth. Spiritual truth here refers to the understanding of our true nature beyond our physical existence and transient emotions. It is the recognition that we are not our thoughts, emotions, or physical bodies, but the consciousness that observes these experiences. When we are caught up in the waves of emotions, we lose sight of this truth. We become identified with our emotional states, forgetting our true nature. This can hinder our spiritual growth and prevent us from experiencing inner peace and contentment. Cultivating emotional balance involves recognizing that we are not our emotions. It involves observing our emotions without judgment, allowing them to rise and fall without getting caught up in them.

Mindfulness practices can be beneficial in cultivating this balance. They help us to stay present and observe our emotions without identification. They enable us to experience our emotions fully, without suppressing or clinging to them.

Social Status

In the societal structure, social status often plays a pivotal role in shaping our identity. It influences our lifestyle, relationships, and even our self-perception. However, while social status is relevant in the societal context, it does not define who we are at the level of pure being. It is important to re-think the relevance of social status and its limitations in defining our true essence.

Social status, defined by factors such as wealth, occupation, education, and family background, is a significant aspect of our societal identity. It often dictates the opportunities we have access to, the circles we interact with, and the way we are perceived by others. In many ways, it shapes our external identity and our interaction with the world. Moreover, social status can influence our self-esteem and self-worth, as societal norms often equate higher status with success. Thus, identification with social status is not only relevant but also impactful on our psychological well-being. Despite its relevance, social status is a superficial layer of our identity. It is transient and subject to change. More importantly, it does not define our intrinsic value or our true essence. At the level of pure being, we are much more than our social status.

Pure being refers to our fundamental essence that exists irrespective of our external circumstances or societal labels. It is our core consciousness, the unchanging and ever-present aspect of ourselves. Identification with social status can often overshadow this pure being, leading us to believe that we are what society defines us to be. Recognizing that we are more than our social status is the first step towards finding balance. It involves understanding that while our social status is a part of our societal identity, it does not encapsulate our entire being. This realization allows us to detach our self-worth from our social status and find value in our intrinsic qualities. It enables us to connect with our pure being, leading to a sense of peace and contentment that is not dependent on external validation.

Moving to I am Presence = Being aware that you exist both 'prior to uttering I AM' and beyond any roles you assume after declaring I AM. Try spending some time knowing yourself without the labels of role and even before you say I Am. The below image will give you an idea of the common roles we identify with. Who would you be without these roles. For some time at least.

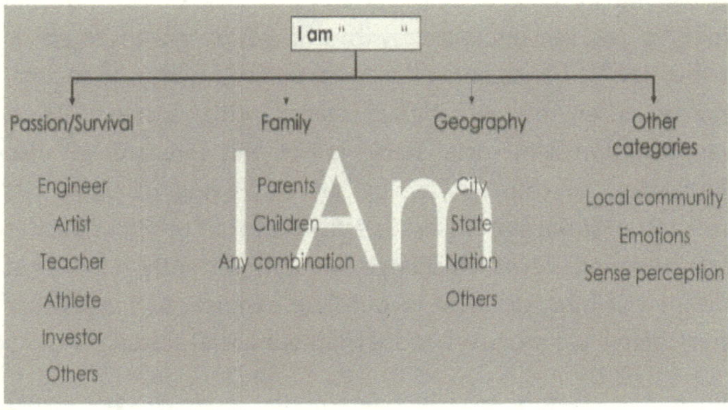

I Am Presence

Human existence is often perceived through the lens of our past experiences and future expectations. However, at the core, we are simply presence - a state of being in the present moment, devoid of past narratives or future anticipations. Simultaneously, we are also witnesses, observing our experiences without judgment. Let us revisit these fundamental aspects of human existence.

Presence refers to the state of being fully engaged in the present moment. It is a state of consciousness where we are not bound by the stories of our past or the expectations of our future. In this state, we experience life as it unfolds, moment by moment. Being present allows us to experience life more fully. It frees us from the constraints of our past and the anxieties of our future. It enables us to engage with our experiences in a more authentic and meaningful way.

Witnessing is the act of observing our experiences without judgment or attachment. As witnesses, we observe our thoughts, emotions, and experiences as they arise and pass, without getting entangled in them. Being a witness allows us to create a space between our experiences and our reactions to them. It enables us to respond to life's situations with more clarity and wisdom, rather than reacting impulsively. Presence and witnessing are two sides of the same coin. When we are present, we naturally become witnesses to our experiences. And when we witness our experiences, we are inherently present in the moment. Being both presence and witness allows us to experience life in its fullness. It enables us to engage with life not as a series of disjointed events, but as a continuous flow of experiences.

Chapter 3

Me and The World

"Words are a pretext. It is the inner bond that draws one person to another, not words." - Rumi

---

In our day-to-day lives, we often perceive ourselves as separate entities in a world that exists outside of us. This perception is largely a result of our sensory experiences and cognitive processes. We see, hear, touch, taste, and smell the world around us, and our conditioned intelligence interprets these sensory inputs in a limited way, creating a sense of self that is distinct from the external world. This sense of separation is not inherently negative. It allows us to navigate the world, make decisions, and interact with others. However, it can also lead to feelings of isolation, disconnection, and a lack of understanding of our place in the world.

Self-enquiry offers a pathway to shift this perception. Through meditation, we can cultivate a state of deep relaxation and focused awareness that will create a space for the Self-enquiry contemplations. As we quiet the mind and turn our attention inward, we begin to observe our voices, emotions, body and world without judgment. In this state of heightened awareness, we can start to see that our sense of self is not fixed or separate, but rather a dynamic and interconnected part of a larger whole. We come to understand that our thoughts, emotions, and sensations are fleeting, appearing and disappearing, some momentarily anchored in space, much like the book you're currently reading and holding. Every experience takes shape within the realm of pure knowing, or simply put, awareness.

As we deepen our meditation practice, we may begin to experience moments of oneness, where the boundary between self and other dissolves. In these moments, we see that we are not separate observers of the world, but rather participants in a vast, interconnected web of life. With an extended practice, we will see that the insight gained during formal meditation minutes, are still valid and available even in the dynamic expression of the waking state. This realization can be both profound and liberating. It can help us to let go of rigid self-concepts and open ourselves to a more fluid and inclusive sense of identity. We see that we are not isolated entities, but integral parts of the universe, arising and subsiding in the same space as everything else.

While our everyday perception often reinforces a sense of separation, meditation along with self-enquiry contemplations offers a pathway to experience the reality of oneness. This shift in perception can have profound implications for how we understand ourselves and our place in the world. It invites us to embrace a more interconnected, compassionate, and holistic view of life. Whether we consciously pursue this state or not, this is what we all seek in the activities every day.

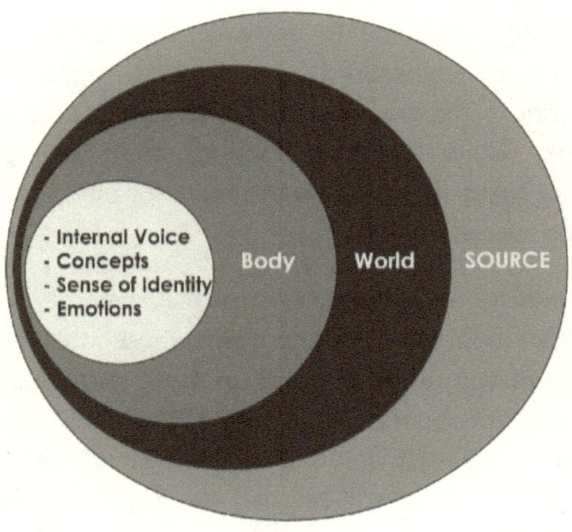

The world of Subject and Objects

From a young age, we are conditioned to perceive the world in terms of subject and object. This is a natural outcome of our cognitive development. As infants, we begin to distinguish between ourselves and our environment, a crucial step in our survival and interaction with the world. This subject-object distinction is reinforced throughout our lives. We identify ourselves as the subject, the observer, and everything else becomes the object of our observation. This dualistic perspective is so ingrained in our cognition that it seems entirely natural and unquestionable.

However, this dualistic way of understanding ourselves and the world is inherently limited. It creates a sense of separation and disconnection, leading to a fragmented view of reality. It can also give rise to feelings of isolation, conflict, and a lack of fulfillment, as we constantly strive to reconcile our inner experiences with the external world. Moreover, there is no explicit teaching from childhood that points out the flaws in this subject-object duality. As a result, we grow up accepting this dualistic perspective as the absolute truth. In contrast to this dualistic perspective, many spiritual traditions propose the concept of non-dual consciousness. This is the understanding that there is no separate self or other, but rather a single, unified field of consciousness.

Non-dual consciousness is not something that can be intellectually understood or conceptualized. It is a direct experience of reality as it is, without the filter of dualistic thinking. In this state, the boundary between subject and object dissolves, revealing the inherent oneness of all existence.

Cultivating non-dual awareness requires a shift from intellectual understanding to direct experience. This often involves practice of meditation, mindfulness, and self-inquiry, which help to quiet the mind and open the heart to the reality of non-dual consciousness. As we let go of our attachment to the subject-object distinction, we begin to experience the world in a new way. We see that the separation between ourselves and the world is an illusion, and that in reality, we are expressions of a single, unified field of consciousness.

Missing the unifying field in duality

The concept of a unifying field that encompasses both the subject (the observer) and the object (the observed) is a profound idea that finds resonance in both modern physics and spirituality. In the realm of quantum physics, the act of observation influences the observed. This is known as the observer effect. The classic example is the double-slit experiment, where light behaves as both a particle and a wave.

However, when one attempts to observe which slit the light goes through, it behaves purely as a particle. This suggests that the observer (subject) and the observed (object) are not separate, but rather interconnected aspects of a unified field.

Field theory, a fundamental construct in physics, also points towards this unity. Fields, such as gravitational or electromagnetic fields, permeate space, influencing the behavior of objects within them. In a sense, objects (like planets or electrons) and the fields they interact with form a unified whole. The subject-object duality dissolves in this context, replaced by a holistic view of reality. In many spiritual traditions, the ultimate reality is described as a state of non-duality, where the perceived separation between the subject and object dissolves. This is often described as a state of oneness or unity consciousness, where the observer and the observed are seen as manifestations of the same underlying reality.

For instance, in Advaita Vedanta, the ultimate reality (Brahman) is considered to be beyond the subject-object duality. Similarly, in Buddhism, the concept of 'Shunyata' or emptiness points towards the interdependence and unity of all phenomena. It is not exactly an empty nothing, but a potential to vibrate and take form. Both physics and spirituality, thus, point towards a unifying field that transcends the subject-object duality. While the language and methodologies differ, the essence is remarkably similar. Physics, through empirical and mathematical investigation, uncovers the fundamental unity of the universe. Spirituality, through introspection and meditation, realizes the inherent oneness of existence.

The concept of a unifying field of subject and object is a powerful idea that bridges science and spirituality. It challenges our usual perception of reality as divided into the observer and the observed, offering instead a vision of profound interconnectedness. As our understanding deepens, both scientifically and spiritually, we may come to fully appreciate the profound implications of this unifying field.

Living the Truth vs. Being Stuck in Stories

Non-duality, the concept of oneness and the absence of an independent self, is a profound philosophical and spiritual idea. However, many people find themselves stuck in the stories and narratives about non-duality, rather than truly living its truth. Let me talk a bit about this paradox. Non-duality, often associated with Eastern philosophies and spiritual traditions, posits that there is no separation between the self and the world. This can be an attractive concept, offering a sense of unity and wholeness.

However, the journey towards understanding and embodying non-duality is not without its challenges. One of the most common pitfalls is getting caught up in the stories and narratives about non-duality. These stories, often filled with mystical and transcendent experiences, can create unrealistic expectations and misconceptions. Many people become so engrossed in these narratives that they overlook the fundamental essence of non-duality: the direct, experiential realization of oneness. They may become stuck in intellectual understanding, without integrating this wisdom into their daily lives.

This disconnect often happens unconsciously. People may believe they are embracing non-duality because they understand it conceptually and can talk about it eloquently. However, living the truth of non-duality requires more than intellectual understanding. It requires a radical shift in perception and a dissolution of deeply ingrained patterns of thought and behavior. Living the truth of non-duality involves seeing through the illusion of separation in every moment. It means recognizing the inherent oneness of all existence, not as a lofty spiritual ideal, but as a lived reality. This requires a deep, experiential understanding that transcends intellectual knowledge and permeates every aspect of life. With sincere inquiry and practice, it is possible to move beyond these stories and truly embody the non-dual reality.

Individuality in Spirituality and the Continuation of Duality

In the realm of spirituality, there is often a focus on unity and oneness, transcending the individual self to experience a greater, universal consciousness. However, this does not negate the importance of acknowledging the different forms of the world and embracing individuality. Let's explore these aspects and discusses how the story of 'me' and the world can continue in duality, even as we delve into spiritual practices.

The world is a tapestry of diverse forms, cultures, perspectives, and experiences. Each form has its unique place and role in the grand scheme of things. Acknowledging this diversity is crucial as it allows us to appreciate the richness and complexity of life. It helps us understand that each individual, each culture, and each form of life contributes to the overall harmony of the world. Spirituality is often associated with transcending the ego or individual self. However, this does not mean that one's individuality is negated or suppressed. On the contrary, genuine spirituality involves embracing and expressing one's unique individuality in alignment with higher consciousness.

Each of us has unique gifts, talents, and perspectives that we bring to the world. Our individuality is an expression of the infinite creativity of the universe. To value our uniqueness in spirituality is to respect our distinct journey and manifestation, all the while acknowledging our link to the greater entirety. Many spiritual customs pivot around the idea of non-duality, which refers to the supreme truth where the apparent divide between oneself and others, or between the observer and the observed, vanishes. However, this does not mean that the play of duality ceases to exist on the relative plane of existence.

Even as we become aware of the non-dual nature of existence, the narrative of 'me' and the world can persist. We can continue to interact with the world, fulfill our roles, and have distinct experiences. The key difference is that we no longer solely identify with the individual self or become entangled in the narratives. Instead, we see them as manifestations of a more profound reality. This reality, which is always accessible, allows us to realize that we are the consciousness, the observer, and are detached from the peaks and valleys of the narrative. We have the freedom to engage with this narrative with any level of intensity we choose to bring forth.

Chapter 4

Limiting Happiness

"The word is not the thing." - Jiddu Krishnamurti

Happiness and fulfillment are deeply personal and subjective experiences that vary greatly from person to person. However, when we confine our sense of joy and satisfaction to only certain activities, we may inadvertently restrict our potential for overall happiness. This chapter explores the direct implications of such self-imposed limitations and discusses how self-realization and awakening can help transcend these imagined limits.

Life is a rich mosaic of experiences, each with its unique potential to bring us joy and fulfillment. When we limit our happiness to select activities, we risk creating a narrow and potentially unfulfilling life experience. For instance, if we derive joy only from our successes and achievements, we may overlook the simple pleasures of life, such as a walk in the park or a good conversation with a friend. This selective approach to happiness can also lead to an overemphasis on certain aspects of life, often at the expense of others. For example, if we find fulfillment only in our work, we may neglect our personal relationships, health, or hobbies. This imbalance can lead to stress, burnout, and a sense of dissatisfaction.

The fallacy in limiting our happiness to select activities can lead us to chase after limited activities or achievements. Moreover, by tying our happiness to specific outcomes, we set ourselves up for disappointment when these outcomes do not materialize. We also create a conditional form of happiness that depends on external circumstances, rather than cultivating an inner sense of joy and contentment.

The process of awakening to our true nature, can help us transcend these imagined limits. It involves recognizing that our true nature is not confined to the ego or the individual self, but is part of a larger, interconnected whole. Through self-realization, we can learn to find happiness and fulfillment in all aspects of life, not just select activities. We can learn to appreciate the inherent value in each moment, whether we're working, spending time with loved ones, or simply enjoying a quiet moment alone.

Being a non-egoic presence helps us understand that happiness is not something to be pursued, but something that arises naturally when we are in alignment with our true nature. It is a state of being, rather than a state of having. It's natural to derive happiness from certain activities, limiting our fulfillment to these activities can be restrictive and counterproductive.

Ego and its expectations

The pursuit of happiness is a universal human endeavor, deeply ingrained in our psyche. However, our unconscious identification with the ego or the separate individual often shapes this pursuit in ways that may not serve our ultimate well-being. It is important to see how the ego influences our quest for happiness and how awakening to our true presence can offer a more fulfilling path.

The ego, in psychological terms, refers to our conscious mind or the part of our identity that we consider our "self." It is the narrator of our life story, the protagonist in our personal drama, and the director of our actions. Unconsciously, we often seek happiness in activities that reinforce this ego identity, especially when playing particular roles in life, such as a parent, a professional, or a friend. For instance, a professional may derive happiness from achievements at work, a parent from the accomplishments of their children, or a friend from the joy of companionship. While there's nothing inherently wrong with these sources of happiness, the problem arises when we limit our happiness to these select activities and roles. This limitation is a direct result of our unconscious habitual identification with the ego.

The ego thrives on control and predictability. It sets expectations and constantly checks for outcomes that align with these expectations. For example, if we identify strongly with our role as a professional, we might set high expectations for career success. We constantly check for outcomes that match these expectations, such as promotions, recognition, or financial rewards. However, this constant checking can rob us of the happiness that can be derived from the process itself. We become so focused on the outcome that we overlook the joy of the journey, the learning opportunities it presents, and the growth it facilitates.

Awakening to our true presence involves realizing that we are more than our ego identities and the roles we play. It is about recognizing that our essence is not separate or isolated but interconnected with the world around us. This realization, often referred to as "awakening," can profoundly shift our approach to happiness. When we awaken to our presence, we understand that happiness is not just about fulfilling the ego's desires or meeting its expectations. Instead, it is about being fully present and engaged in every moment, regardless of the activity we are involved in or the role we are playing. It is about finding joy in the process rather than being solely focused on the outcome.

Our unconscious identification with the ego can limit our pursuit of happiness, awakening to our true presence offers a path to a more profound and enduring form of fulfillment. By transcending the ego's expectations and control, we can learn to derive happiness from the richness of our experiences rather than the attainment of specific outcomes. This shift in perspective can transform our approach to happiness, making it a state of being rather than a fleeting experience dependent on external circumstances. One can make use of the below image to check their state of presence at any moment, if it is dominated by ego or, if you are in a state of pure presence.

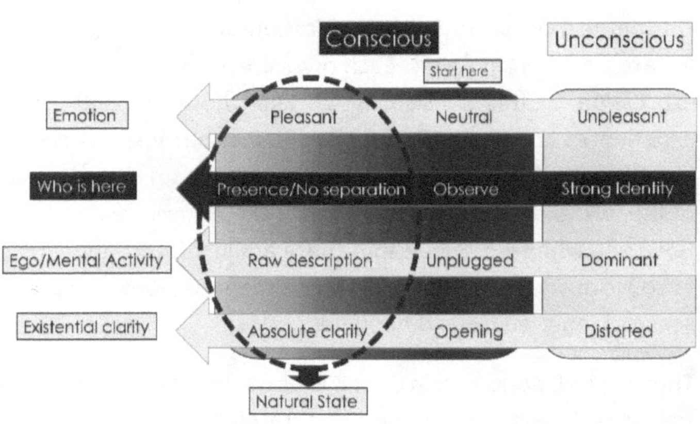

Absolute Happiness is Self-Realisation

The absolute happiness we seek may be more closely linked to our understanding of ourselves as consciousness appearing in different forms. From a young age, we are taught to seek happiness in the external world. We chase after success, strive for positive relationships, and engage in activities that bring us joy. While these pursuits can certainly contribute to our sense of well-being, they often offer only temporary happiness. Once the initial excitement fades, we find ourselves seeking the next source of pleasure or fulfillment.

Consciousness, in its simplest form, refers to our awareness or perception of reality. It is the underlying essence of who we are, beyond our physical bodies, thoughts, and emotions. When we realize that we are fundamentally consciousness, our perspective on happiness begins to shift. We recognize that our true nature as consciousness is inherently peaceful, content, and unconditioned by the external world. This realization can lead to a sense of absolute happiness that is independent of our activities and relationships.

One of the most profound aspects of consciousness is its ability to take on different forms. Each of us, in our uniqueness, is an expression of this consciousness. Our thoughts, body, and experiences are all manifestations of consciousness. When we identify with these forms, we often get caught up in the drama of life, we experience pleasure and pain, success and failure. However, when we realize that these are just forms appearing in consciousness, we can experience them without losing our sense of inner peace and happiness.

The absolute happiness we seek is not a fleeting emotion or a transient state of mind. It is our natural state as consciousness.

When we realize this, we no longer depend on our activities and relationships for happiness. Instead, we find a deep sense of joy and fulfillment in simply being. This does not mean that we stop engaging in activities or nurturing relationships. Rather, it means that we do so from a place of fullness rather than lack. We participate in life fully, without being swayed by the ups and downs of our experiences.

Not necessarily laughing

There is often a misconception that being happy equates to constantly laughing or maintaining a state of bliss. While laughter and bliss can be expressions of happiness, they are not its sole indicators. In the diversified world we live in, happiness is a multifaceted experience that is deeply intertwined with an intelligence sourced in peace and clarity. Let us explore this nuanced understanding of happiness.

Laughter is often seen as a universal sign of happiness. Similarly, a state of bliss is frequently associated with a high degree of happiness. However, equating happiness solely with laughter and bliss can lead to a skewed understanding of what it means to be truly happy.

Life is a complex set of experiences when we try to employ only the thinking mind, encompassing a wide range of emotions and states of being. It is unrealistic and potentially harmful to expect oneself to maintain a constant state of laughter or bliss. Such expectations can lead to feelings of inadequacy or failure when one's emotional experience does not align with these narrow definitions of happiness. In the current world scenario, marked by rapid changes, uncertainty, and a plethora of challenges, happiness cannot be confined to mere laughter or bliss. Happiness, in this context, involves resilience, adaptability, and the ability to find peace amidst chaos.

It involves finding joy in small, everyday experiences, cultivating a sense of gratitude, and maintaining a positive outlook despite adversities. It also involves fostering healthy relationships, pursuing meaningful goals, and contributing to the well-being of others. At the heart of this broader understanding of happiness lies an intelligence that is sourced in peace and clarity. This intelligence goes beyond the cognitive abilities typically associated with the term. It involves a deep understanding of oneself and the world, a sense of inner peace, and the clarity to navigate life's complexities with grace and wisdom.

This intelligence allows us to respond to life's challenges with equanimity, make decisions that align with our values. It enables us to connect with others in a genuine and compassionate manner if called for, contributing to our own happiness and the happiness of those around us.

Causeless Happiness

The journey of self-realization and the practice of mindfulness can lead us to a state of causeless happiness, where we find joy in simply being alive and experiencing the world. This is a state of joy that does not depend on external factors or conditions. We appreciate the miracle of existence and the beauty of the world around us. We experience a sense of awe and wonder that transcends our ordinary perceptions of reality. As we peel away the layers of our conditioned self, we begin to experience our true nature, which is inherently peaceful, content, and free from suffering.

Before awakening, our sense of happiness is often tied to the ego. The ego, which identifies with the body, mind, and emotions, seeks happiness in external conditions. In contrast, when we awaken to our true self, we tap into this reservoir of causeless happiness. We realize that happiness is not something to be pursued outside of us, but it is our very nature.

Causeless happiness is It is not affected by the ups and downs of life. Instead, it allows us to remain centered and peaceful amidst the changing tides of life. Living from a place of causeless happiness does not mean that we stop engaging with the world or become indifferent to our experiences. On the contrary, we engage with life more fully and authentically. We experience emotions, work towards our goals, and participate in life's activities. However, we do so without losing touch with our inner peace and happiness. We understand that our true nature is inherently peaceful and content, and we don't need to depend on external circumstances for our happiness. This understanding frees us from the endless chase after transient pleasures and allows us to find joy in every moment.

Part 2 – The Grand Discovery

Chapter 5

The Path of Science

"The limits of my language mean the limits of my world." - Ludwig Wittgenstein

---

One of the grandest pursuits in science is the search for a 'Theory of Everything' - a single, all-encompassing, coherent theoretical framework that can explain and link together all physical aspects of the universe. This theory aims to unite the realms of general relativity (which describes gravity and the large-scale structure of the universe) and quantum mechanics (which explains the behavior of particles at the smallest scales).

Despite significant progress, a complete Theory of Everything remains elusive. The challenge lies in reconciling the seemingly incompatible descriptions of the universe provided by general relativity and quantum mechanics. Nevertheless, the pursuit continues, driven by the belief that such a unifying theory exists. Another major quest in science is understanding the origins of the universe. The Big Bang theory, which posits that the universe began as a hot, dense point nearly 13.8 billion years ago, is currently the best explanation we have. However, it leaves unanswered questions, such as what caused the Big Bang, and what (if anything) existed before it.

In an attempt to answer these questions, scientists are delving into realms like quantum cosmology and string theory. They are also studying cosmic microwave background radiation - the afterglow of the Big Bang - to gather clues about the universe's infancy. The question of consciousness - what it is, how it arises, and why it exists - is another profound mystery that science seeks to unravel. Despite advances in neuroscience and cognitive science, consciousness remains largely enigmatic.

Some scientists and philosophers argue that consciousness might be a fundamental aspect of the universe, much like space and time. Others propose that consciousness emerges from complex computation among brain neurons. While we do not yet have a definitive answer, the quest to understand consciousness pushes the boundaries of science and prompts us to reconsider our view of the universe.

The Dualistic Approach

Science, in its quest to understand the universe, has traditionally adopted a dualistic approach. This approach, rooted in the separation of the observer and the observed, has been instrumental in numerous scientific advancements. However, when it comes to addressing existential questions, this dualistic perspective may encounter certain limitations. The dualistic perspective in science is characterized by the distinction between the subject (the observer) and the object (the observed). This separation is fundamental to the scientific method. Scientists observe phenomena, conduct experiments, and analyze results objectively, maintaining a clear distinction between the observer and the observed.

This approach has led to remarkable discoveries and advancements in various fields of science, from physics and chemistry to biology and astronomy. It has enabled us to decode the laws of nature, understand the workings of living organisms, and unravel the mysteries of the cosmos. Despite its successes, the dualistic approach of science encounters limitations when grappling with existential questions. These are questions that relate to the nature of existence, the purpose of life, the concept of consciousness, and the ultimate reality.

One of the reasons for these limitations is that existential questions often delve into realms that transcend the observable physical universe. For instance, questions about consciousness, subjective experiences, or the nature of reality challenge the conventional boundaries of scientific inquiry.

Moreover, existential questions often involve aspects of reality that are not easily measurable or quantifiable. They touch upon the profound mystery of existence that may not be fully comprehensible through objective analysis alone. To address these existential questions, a more holistic approach may be needed, one that transcends the dualistic perspective. Such an approach would not discard the valuable tools of science but would expand them to include subjective experiences and introspective insights. This approach recognizes that the observer and the observed are not entirely separate but are interconnected aspects of a unified whole. It acknowledges that subjective experiences, such as consciousness, are integral parts of reality and need to be studied as such.

In the realm of human understanding, science has always held a unique position. It is seen as a beacon of truth, a source of answers to our existential questions, and a tool for technological and engineering advancements. This trust in science is not unfounded; it is based on its dualistic nature, which combines theoretical principles with practical applications. However, it is essential to acknowledge that science, like any other field, has its limitations. Science operates on two fundamental levels: the theoretical and the practical. Theoretical science seeks to understand the natural world and its phenomena, while practical science, often manifested as technology and engineering, applies this understanding to solve "real"-world problems.

This dualistic nature of science has led to numerous technological advancements that have significantly improved our quality of life. From the invention of the wheel to the development of the internet, science has been instrumental in shaping human civilization. The success of practical science in creating tangible improvements in our lives has fostered a deep-seated trust in the scientific process. People look to science for answers to existential questions because they see the results of scientific inquiry all around them. This trust is not just based on faith; it is a promissory trust, grounded in the proven ability of science to deliver results. Despite its many successes, science has its limitations. It operates within the confines of our current understanding of the universe, which is continually evolving. What we accept as scientific truth today may be disproved or refined tomorrow as our knowledge expands.

Moreover, science can only answer questions that can be empirically tested and validated. Questions about morality, aesthetics, and other subjective experiences often fall outside the purview of science. Here are some examples of the limitations of science:

Subjectivity of Experience: Science relies on empirical evidence, which can be observed and measured. However, it struggles to explain subjective experiences, such as emotions, thoughts, and consciousness, which are inherently personal and cannot be objectively measured.

Moral and Ethical Questions: Science can provide data and information, but it cannot determine what is morally or ethically right or wrong. These decisions often involve personal beliefs, cultural norms, or philosophical considerations that are beyond the scope of scientific inquiry.

Theoretical Limitations: Some scientific theories, while widely accepted, have limitations. For example, the theory of relativity and quantum mechanics, two pillars of modern physics, are incompatible at certain scales, indicating a limitation in our current understanding of the universe.

Scope of Study: Science can only study phenomena that are observable and measurable. Phenomena that do not interact with our observable universe, or do so in ways that we cannot currently measure, are beyond the reach of science.

Changing Paradigms: Scientific understanding is not static; it evolves over time. What is considered a scientific fact today may be disproved or modified in the future as new evidence emerges or as investigative techniques improve.

Remember, these limitations do not undermine the value of science. Instead, they highlight the need for an inclusive approach to understanding subjective fundamental experiences, one that includes but is not limited to scientific inquiry.

What is the highest knowledge you can gain?

Is it the study of geology? Or the intricacies of human biology? Or perhaps the subject in which you specialize?

As humans, our ability to question enables us to delve deep into the study of any phenomenon we encounter or experience. It's our innate curiosity to comprehend why things are the way they are that propels us towards expertise. In this journey of exploration, we aspire to find satisfying answers for observed phenomena. Answers that are fulfilling enough to trace the chain of causality back to the bedrock of science, religion, or some form of philosophy or ideology.

There are myriad reasons why one might seek knowledge. It could be because their profession necessitates it, or because they desire validation from a group, or because they believe they can be a source of information contributing to the well-being of others, or simply because they want to demonstrate to the world their capacity to learn anything they wish. However, there are limits to what we can understand and learn about the world.

The narrative of the contemporary world offers limited areas of interest for exploration. It could be socio-political-economic deductions and studies, keeping oneself informed about the trajectory of societal well-being. The scientific pursuit of evidence, which we monitor, hoping that a new discovery will help resolve humanitarian crises, alleviate suffering on Earth, and perhaps, provide the ultimate answer to our existential questions. Then there's the realm of faith, where we acknowledge the mystery of creation and the human form. However, we conveniently resort to this belief system when the situation calls for it (out of fear or reverence). And then there's this other category, which holds the key to attaining the highest wisdom and knowledge a human being can access. Allow me to articulate a beautiful, simple, and rational way to enter this pristine space, where you can embrace the duality of beauty and ugliness, good and evil, anger and compassion.

The knowledge of knowing you are alive. Yes, you can start here if you haven't already. Over time, we may have unconsciously taken this for granted. This will be the greatest service we as individuals can render to ourselves and society in a single lifetime. The simple fact that you are here, reading these lines and curves that we call letters, words, and sentences, and deriving meaning that represents an experience of the world, is astounding. While we may begin alluding to concepts that other categories have discovered, please note that even in the scenario of failing to explain the observations, you would still be alive and accessing your intuition.

I'm not suggesting that we've got it all wrong; the current narrative of politics, science, religion, and art are all ways to express our zeal and motivation to survive and feel alive. I'm rather suggesting that we should directly go to the source of all these peripheral activities and express from there. That knowing, which doesn't require you to remember paragraphs, concepts, and scriptures. Rather, that knowing which is the source of every scripture that we have written. You may use your language to express this highest knowing, however, this highest knowledge is not a combination of words. It is an insight, the one insight which we as humans have access to at any point. You may consider reading and listening about them, from any phenomenal source. However, it doesn't mean a thing if you are not seeing it for yourself.

The easy and evident approach to gain this highest insight is to simply make use of your ability to observe (anything) and ask questions. Now the trick here is to ask the question more responsibly and make sure that it is honestly translating the experience you are trying to find the answer for. Or simply put, you have to mean it when you ask.

There are a few questions which, when contemplated, will initiate a sequence of detonations within, one that will not harm you but will break all your hollow and narrow belief systems in time. Some questions are: who is here right now, experiencing the body sensations? Who is hearing the voice that is reading this word? Can I know anything without me being here? Are there two things here, me and the world? Who is the one who understands the concepts? Etc. You don't have to go through all, but pick one existential question that resonates with your thirst to understand the absolute nature of you or the world around you.

You can slowly and gracefully and with honesty explore your way. Your way to that place where all of your contemplation and sensory experiences are taking place. You can make use of awareness exercises, meditation, and mindfulness ways. I am not trying to point you to some otherworldly experience that holds very little to no value for the life we are living. No, I am pointing you to that very fabric on which this thriving life of ours is built. And we need to start behaving from this space, which is not a mystery or attainable to only a few renounced humans.

If there is one capital 'T' truth which is the source of everything on earth and any universe, it should be here right now and in every now to come. Gaining the knowledge of this highest is equal to being this knowledge itself. Your thoughts about your body and the world dictate whether you wish to find satisfaction in knowing the finite causality of this world or if you choose to live from the ultimate cause of ALL. ONE says, what do you know when you know nothing? Meaning, for a while if you keep aside all that you know about who you are, what this world is according to science, philosophy, or religion, etc. EVERY concept dropped. What do you know now?

Do this for a few seconds, you will notice the sounds around you, you will see the solid world, you will have the field of body sensations, or simply put, there is a raw perception of the 3D world. This raw perception nowhere says I am a unique experience in my own right as a separate object. When you observe your body, thoughts, and world in a non-judgmental space, you will start entering that unifying field in which the story of Earth and other universes is continuously unfolding. It is ridiculously non-personal; we think that expanding our boundary by one or two layers makes us inclusive and considerate. No, as long as you see a conditional boundary, we will continue to evolve in order through chaos. And I have to admit, it is my intuition which also says, it is a natural course of evolution in consciousness. The chaos we create is a reflection of our mental state as a species. A reflection of the confusion we manifest in the physical form.

The Subject in Scientific Inquiry

The role of the subject in scientific inquiry is often overlooked in favor of objective, empirical data. However, the subject's importance cannot be understated, particularly when exploring the intersection of quantum physics and spiritual inquiry. It's worthwhile to talk a bit about the significance of the subject in scientific inquiry and how a quantum approach can unify scientific and spiritual exploration.

Traditional science places a strong emphasis on objectivity, often sidelining the subject's role. The observer is considered separate from the observed, and the focus is on gathering empirical, reproducible data. This approach has led to significant advancements in our understanding of the natural world. However, it often overlooks the influence of the observer on the observed, an aspect that is crucial in certain fields of study, particularly quantum physics. Quantum physics challenges the traditional notion of an objective reality independent of the observer. In the quantum realm, the act of observation influences the observed, blurring the line between the subject and the object. This phenomenon, known as the observer effect, underscores the importance of the subject in scientific inquiry.

For instance, the famous double-slit experiment demonstrates that light behaves as a particle or a wave depending on whether it is observed. This experiment highlights the integral role of the observer in determining the nature of reality at the quantum level.

The observer-centric view of quantum physics resonates with many spiritual traditions, which emphasize the interconnectedness of all things and the central role of consciousness in shaping reality. Both quantum physics and spiritual inquiry suggest that the observer and the observed are not separate but are part of a unified whole.

This perspective opens up new avenues for a unified approach to scientific and spiritual inquiry. It suggests that our understanding of the universe is not just shaped by objective facts but also by our subjective experiences and consciousness. The subject's role in scientific inquiry is not just important but indispensable, particularly when viewed from a quantum-spiritual perspective. Recognizing this can lead to a more holistic approach to understanding the universe, one that harmonizes scientific investigation with spiritual exploration. This unified approach acknowledges the interplay between the observer and the observed, offering a more comprehensive understanding of reality that transcends the traditional boundaries of science and spirituality.

A Shift in Scientific Paradigm

The study of consciousness has long been a contentious issue in the scientific community. The current scientific paradigm, with its emphasis on empirical data and objective observation, often sidelines consciousness as a subjective phenomenon that is beyond the scope of scientific inquiry. This part explores how this denial of consciousness and the brain-centric approach could potentially stall the evolution of science and how the confusion between the brain and consciousness poses a significant challenge.

The prevailing scientific paradigm is rooted in physicalism, the belief that everything, including consciousness, can be reduced to physical processes. This perspective has led to a brain-centric approach to studying consciousness, with scientists seeking to locate consciousness within the brain's neural networks. However, consciousness, by its very nature, is subjective and cannot be observed or measured in the same way as physical phenomena. By denying or ignoring consciousness, science risks overlooking a crucial aspect of human experience. This denial could potentially stall the evolution of science, preventing it from moving towards a more holistic understanding of reality.

The brain-centric approach to studying consciousness assumes that the brain generates consciousness. However, this perspective may be misleading. It is akin to confusing the reflection of the moon in a pond for the moon itself.

While the brain is undoubtedly involved in the manifestation of conscious experience, it may not be the source of consciousness. Instead, the brain could be a conduit or a reflector, facilitating the expression of consciousness in the physical world but not producing it.

This confusion between the brain and consciousness has led to what is often referred to as the "hard problem" of consciousness - the question of how physical processes in the brain give rise to subjective conscious experiences. However, this "problem" arises from the assumption that consciousness is a product of the brain, an assumption that is increasingly being questioned. The limitations of the current scientific paradigm and the challenges posed by the study of consciousness call for a shift in perspective. This shift involves moving away from a purely brain-centric approach towards a consciousness-centric paradigm.

A consciousness-centric paradigm acknowledges consciousness as a fundamental aspect of reality, not just a byproduct of physical processes. It opens up new avenues for scientific inquiry, incorporating subjective experiences into the realm of scientific exploration. This shift does not undermine the achievements of physicalist science; instead, it expands upon them, integrating subjective and objective aspects of reality into a more comprehensive, holistic framework.

Chapter 6

The Path of Religion

"The more the words, the less the meaning, and how does that profit anyone?" - Ecclesiastes 6:11

Religion has been a fundamental part of human societies for millennia, providing a framework for understanding the world and our place in it. For many, religious teachings offer solace and comfort, acting as a sanctuary for the mind that seeks higher truths. However, while religion can provide a temporary resting place, it may not be the ultimate answer to the union that humans seek in their spiritual evolution.

Religious teachings often address existential questions and the mysteries of life, offering interpretations and narratives that help individuals make sense of their experiences. These teachings can act as a solace for those who are aware of a higher truth and are on a quest to understand it. The rituals and prayers found in various religions can provide a sense of peace and tranquility, helping individuals cope with life's challenges and uncertainties.

Religion also offers a sense of community and belonging, which can be comforting for those on a spiritual journey. The shared beliefs and practices can create a sense of unity and mutual understanding, providing further solace for the seeking mind. Each religion offers a particular perspective on life, divinity, and the nature of reality, and these perspectives can vary widely. Therefore, an individual's spiritual journey might not be fully encompassed within a single religious framework.

Moreover, religious teachings are often interpreted literally, which can limit their scope and depth. The symbolic and metaphorical aspects of these teachings, which can offer profound insights into the nature of existence, are sometimes overlooked. This can lead to a rigid and dogmatic understanding of religion, which can hinder rather than facilitate spiritual growth. The journey of spiritual evolution involves a continuous exploration and understanding of the self and the universe. This journey is deeply personal and unique to each individual, and it may not be fully captured within the confines of organized religion.

Spiritual evolution often involves transcending traditional religious boundaries and embracing a more holistic and inclusive understanding of divinity and existence. It is about recognizing the interconnectedness of all life and the inherent divinity within each individual.

While religion can provide a starting point and a temporary resting place in this journey, the ultimate union that humans seek may lie beyond religious doctrines and dogmas. This union is often experienced as a profound sense of oneness with all existence, a state of consciousness that transcends dualities and separateness.

Distinguishing Religion from Spirituality

The terms 'religion' and 'spirituality' are often used interchangeably, but they represent two distinct yet interconnected aspects of human experience. Understanding the difference between them is crucial for personal growth and the pursuit of existential truth. Let us look into why it's important to distinguish religion from spirituality and how spirituality transcends religious stories and beliefs to touch the essence of religious teachings.

Religion is typically defined by a set of beliefs, rituals, and moral codes shared by a community. It often involves worship of a higher power or deity and adherence to a specific doctrine or scripture. Religion provides a structured approach to spirituality, offering a sense of belonging and a communal way of celebrating and making sense of the mysteries of life.

Spirituality, on the other hand, is a more individual and personal experience. It involves a deep sense of connection with the self, others, nature, and the universe as a whole. Spirituality transcends religious boundaries and dogmas, focusing on personal growth, self-discovery, and the pursuit of inner peace and enlightenment. Distinguishing religion from spirituality is important for several reasons:

Personal Freedom: Spirituality allows for personal freedom and self-expression that may not be possible within the confines of a specific religious doctrine. It enables individuals to explore their own beliefs and experiences without being bound by prescribed rituals or beliefs.

Inclusivity: Spirituality is inclusive and universal, transcending religious, cultural, and geographical boundaries. It promotes unity and interconnectedness, fostering a sense of global community and shared humanity.

Personal Growth: Spirituality encourages introspection, self-awareness, and personal growth. It emphasizes the importance of personal experience and inner wisdom, promoting self-discovery and personal transformation.

While religious teachings often rely on stories and beliefs to convey moral and spiritual lessons, spirituality goes beyond these narratives to touch the essence of these teachings. It focuses on the underlying themes of love, compassion, forgiveness, and unity that are at the heart of most religious teachings. Spirituality encourages direct experience and personal interpretation, allowing individuals to connect with these universal truths in their own unique way. It recognizes that while stories and beliefs can point the way, the truth must be experienced directly to be fully understood.

The common-sense Spirituality, before concepts

Anyone entering this domain of exploration may encounter the immensity and baffling aspects of awakening. It's equally important to acknowledge and include the life we knew before realization. This inclusion should be a loving and truly compassionate approach towards society.

The causality is very clear as to why the majority of humanity is living a compartmentalized and divided life. It becomes the responsibility of the seers to remain humble and not make spirituality sound too mysterious or available to a select few. The beauty and essence of spirituality is that you see how simple and direct self-realization is.

What the world calls Moksha, Nirvana, Awakening, etc. is that simple recognition of who you are without the baggage of your story. What do you see when you rest the narrator? I call this common sense, because you are not supposed to study or do PhDs on how to be alive.

A very important aspect to remember is that when one embarks on the path of spirituality, you should not start with the denial of the existing paradigm. Paradigm of science's way to know the world or religion's way of dealing with the unknown. All of these are the avenues we, as an aware, intelligent, curious species, choose to find reassurance of not being alone, intuitively sensing something or some force behind the world we see.

What is the common thread that weaves through every moment of every human? The simple fact that you are alive and breathing. The forgotten fact (almost all the time) that you are alive in the world you woke up to this morning. And aware of the concepts you learn, which is you trying to rationalize the behavior of the world.

You can be aware of the environment, wherever you are right now. You do not have to think first and then start with a perception. Of course, you have to give your attention to a perception consciously. This awareness is the same for every person or living being irrespective of the background.

The word in question has gained some bad reputation and has misled the seeking population over the last couple of decades, I would say. Which begs me to isolate spirituality from religion. For religious institutions were successful in boosting the ego of supremacy, as to who owns the truth, however, the Truth itself wouldn't care less about the stories we use to bury the essence of every religion.

Henceforth, it becomes the prime responsibility of me and every other being who wants to express the essence of spirituality, to make minimal and simple use of language. So that we can communicate the highest wisdom that is timeless and more importantly, non-religious. You may choose to integrate and respect other faiths after you have found yourself living a life in Truth.

You can forget about the term spirituality altogether, for good. If needed, you can choose to use this term in the future. I never sought after to master or learn spirituality, rather an approach of Truth for truth's sake. The current day marketing strategy involves selling the services using the perks or side effects of spiritual awakening. That is using peace, calm, happiness, etc., to promote a service.

This is alright as long as one makes it clear before, or at least during the course of the program/teaching, that the ultimate goal of any spiritual practice is self-realisation or realising the one consciousness when in human form. The One consciousness which plays the role of a manifest entity, taking the form of human biology to witness impersonally and experience the potential it has to eternally create.

Please make sure you do not associate spirituality with any religion or person or form. Do not worry or argue with yourself and others about who came first, whom did God speak to first, or which civilization got it First. Whoever had this realisation in the timeline, the pristine truth which was discovered is very much the same and available now as well. Make use of the senses you have, the perception of the world, and your ability to ask Existential questions: Who am I without the story? What do I know for sure about the waking state? Does reality care what I think the reality is? Etc.

Any question that is not serving your personal desire and goals. Even if you follow the line of personal desires, you can still navigate to the space of the same realisation and awakened space. But it will be a longer and inefficient route.

Become the curious child, an honest and open-minded adult when you contemplate. This is the common-sense approach towards seeking truth for truth's sake/spirituality. Which only depends on what you see within and experience, and not what others have to say.

The perpetuation of duality

Religious beliefs can sometimes perpetuate a sense of duality and limit our understanding of God or Higher Truth to specific forms, potentially delaying the collective awakening of humanity. At the heart of many religious teachings is the concept of duality: good versus evil, sacred versus profane, divine versus human. This dichotomy can provide a moral framework and help followers navigate life's complexities. However, it can also perpetuate a sense of separation and division, both within the individual and in society.

The duality inherent in religious beliefs can create an 'us versus them' mentality, fostering division and conflict. It can also lead to a dualistic perception of oneself, separating the spiritual self from the physical self. This sense of separation can hinder the realization of our inherent wholeness and unity with the universe, delaying the collective awakening of humanity.

Religions often depict God or Higher Truth in specific forms or images, providing followers with a tangible representation of the divine. While these forms can facilitate devotion and worship, they can also limit our understanding and experience of the divine.

By associating God or Higher Truth with specific forms, we risk confining the infinite and formless nature of the divine to our limited human perceptions. This can lead to a narrow and rigid understanding of the divine, preventing us from experiencing the boundless nature of Higher Truth. The perpetuation of duality and the limitation of the divine to specific forms can delay the collective awakening of humanity. Collective awakening refers to the realization of our inherent unity and interconnectedness, transcending the illusion of separation and duality.

Fear or Reverence

Religion, in its traditional form, often uses the concepts of reward and punishment to guide moral behavior. The fear of divine wrath or the desire for divine favor can be powerful motivators for adherence to religious doctrines. This fear-based approach can be effective in maintaining social order, but it can also lead to an external, rather than internal, motivation for ethical behavior.

Personal desires also play a significant role in religious practices. Many religions promise rewards, both in this life and the afterlife, for those who follow their teachings. These promises can range from material prosperity to eternal salvation, appealing to deep-seated human desires for security, happiness, and the avoidance of suffering. While these aspects of religion can provide comfort and a sense of order, they can also limit spiritual growth. The focus on fear and personal desires can distract from the pursuit of self-transcendence and unconditional love, which are at the heart of spiritual evolution.

In contrast to the fear and desire-based approach of religion, spirituality centers around reverence for a higher power. This reverence is not born out of fear of punishment or desire for reward, but out of a deep sense of awe and wonder for the mystery of existence. Spirituality encourages a direct, personal connection with the divine, transcending religious dogmas and rituals. It emphasizes the transformative power of love, compassion, and selfless service, promoting an inner transformation that reflects in one's actions and interactions.

The spiritual approach to God is not about appeasing a divine entity but about realizing our inherent divinity and unity with all existence. It is about transcending the illusion of separateness and experiencing the interconnectedness of all life. Religion and spirituality can both play a role in our spiritual journey, they offer different paths. Religion, with its focus on fear and personal desires, provides a structured approach to morality and a sense of belonging. However, it can also limit our spiritual growth if we become too attached to the rewards and punishments it promises. In the end, both religion and spirituality can guide us on our journey, but it is up to us to choose the path that resonates with our inner truth.

Chapter 7

The Independent Truth

"The quieter you become, the more you can hear." - Ram Dass

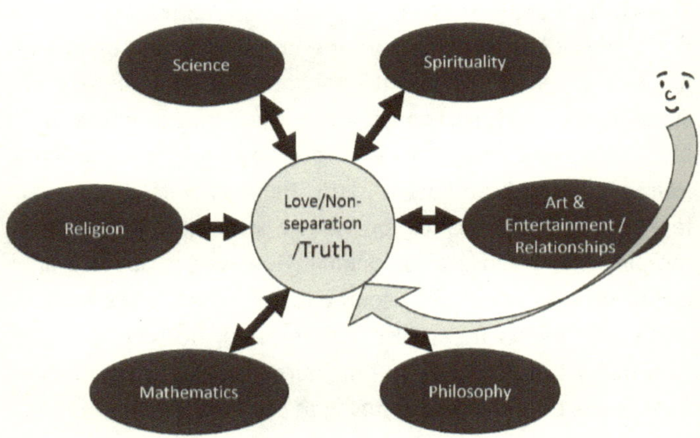

Human beings, regardless of their formal education or conditioning by beliefs, possess an innate ability to sense the mystery of existence and explore the nature of who we are and the world around us. This inherent curiosity and wonder have been the driving force behind our evolution, shaping our understanding of ourselves and our place in the universe. From the earliest days of our species, humans have looked at the world with a sense of awe and wonder. The vastness of the sky, the rhythm of the seasons, the complexity of life - all these have stirred in us a profound sense of mystery. This sense of mystery is not dependent on formal education or specific beliefs; it is a fundamental part of our human nature.

Our ability to sense this mystery is what compels us to ask questions, to seek answers, to explore the unknown. It is what drives us to climb mountains, dive into the depths of the ocean, and reach for the stars. It is also what prompts us to delve into the depths of our own consciousness, seeking to understand who we are and why we are here.

Our exploration of the world is not limited to the physical realm. We also seek to understand the intangible aspects of existence - emotions, thoughts, consciousness, and the sense of self. We ponder questions like: What does it mean to be human? What is the nature of reality?

These explorations are not confined to those with formal education or specific beliefs. They are undertaken by all humans, regardless of their background or circumstances. A farmer tilling the soil, a musician composing a melody, a child gazing at the stars - all are engaged in this exploration, driven by their innate curiosity and their sense of the mystery of existence. While formal education and conditioning by beliefs can shape our understanding of the world, they are not prerequisites for sensing the mystery of existence or exploring our nature and the world. In fact, they can sometimes limit our exploration, confining it within predefined frameworks and established norms.

The true exploration of existence transcends formal education and conditioning by beliefs. It involves an open mind, a willingness to question, and the courage to venture into the unknown. It is about embracing uncertainty, tolerating ambiguity, and finding joy in the journey of discovery.

Reality does not care what we think and believe about its nature

The quest to understand the nature of who we are and the world around us is as old as humanity itself. The truth about our nature and the world is what it IS, independent of our thoughts, beliefs, or perceptions. It remains constant, unchanging, and universal, regardless of our mental constructs.

Truth, in its purest form, is independent and unchanging. It does not alter based on our thoughts, beliefs, or perceptions. Our understanding or interpretation of the truth may change, but the truth itself remains constant. This is the fundamental nature of truth - it is what it IS.

Our thoughts, beliefs, and perceptions are shaped by our experiences, conditioning, and the societal and cultural contexts we live in. They are subjective and can vary greatly from person to person. However, they do not change the underlying truth. They merely provide different lenses through which we view and interpret the truth. The journey towards truth is a process of peeling away the layers of our mental constructs to reveal the underlying reality. It involves questioning our beliefs, challenging our perceptions, and being open to new experiences and perspectives.

This journey can be undertaken through various paths - science, philosophy, spirituality, art, or personal introspection, to name a few. Each path offers a different approach to exploring the truth, but they all lead to the same destination - the realization of the independent, unchanging truth. The discovery of the independent truth is a grand and transformative experience. It changes our understanding of ourselves and the world around us. It brings clarity, wisdom, and a deep sense of peace and contentment. It allows us to see beyond the illusions of separateness and duality, revealing the interconnectedness and unity of all existence.

This grand discovery is not a one-time event but a continuous process of growth and evolution. As we continue to explore and understand the truth, we deepen our connection with ourselves and the world around us. We become more compassionate, more aware, and more in tune with the underlying reality.

Witnessing the Phenomenal

The journey towards self-realization is a profound and transformative process. It involves becoming a witness to our phenomenal experiences, meditating to cultivate awareness, and seeking the highest truth through pure experience. The first step towards self-realization is becoming a witness to our phenomenal experiences. This involves observing our thoughts, emotions, and sensations without judgment or identification. As we cultivate this witness consciousness, we begin to see that we are not our thoughts or emotions, but the awareness that perceives them.

This shift in perspective allows us to experience life more fully and directly. We begin to see the world as it is, not as we think it is. We realize that our perceptions are often colored by our beliefs, expectations, and past experiences, and that the truth lies beyond these mental constructs. Meditation is a vital practice in the journey towards self-realization. It cultivates mindfulness and presence, allowing us to become more aware of our phenomenal experiences. Through meditation, we master the ability to observe and tune into the present moment, where the highest truth resides.

Initially, meditation will require formal practice. We may need to set aside specific times for meditation and use techniques to focus the mind. However, as we deepen our practice, meditation becomes less of a formal activity and more of a natural state of being. We find ourselves remaining in a meditative state even amidst the hustle and bustle of daily life. The ultimate proof of self-realization is not found in intellectual understanding or belief, but in self-evident experience. This experience is not colored by our beliefs or the limited intelligence of the ego. It is a direct, unmediated experience of the highest truth.

When we experience the world in this way, we realize that we are not separate, isolated entities, but integral parts of a unified whole. We see that the same life force that flows through us flows through all of existence. This realization brings a sense of peace, joy, interconnectedness and patience for the humanity to correct its course, that transcends our ordinary experiences. While recognizing ourselves as witnesses is a crucial step, it is not the end of the journey. To complete the process of self-realization, we must also include the phenomenal world in our awareness. This is where the practice of mindfulness comes in.

Mindfulness involves being fully present and engaged in the current moment. It means paying attention to our experiences, both internal and external, without judgment or distraction. Through mindfulness, we learn to embrace the phenomenal world, seeing it as an integral part of our existence rather than something separate or alien. This realization brings us closer to the state of self-realization.

Language is not the experience. Pure Knowing Is

Separating words and imagination with the actual experience in the world

We often take language, and our ability to express ourselves, for granted. At times, we utter words that are not well-thought-out or accurate. Language should reflect an emotional state, an opinion, or an observation of the world without bias or distortion. The aim of this section is to separate language, which is supposed to represent an experience in the world, from the experience itself. This separation allows us to appreciate the beauty of an experience more, rather than being mentally lost in the translation of the experience and constantly thinking about how to express it. In the above image, the physical reality is a magnificent mountain. For communication purposes the symbol 'M o u n t a i n' represents this shape and form, which exists prior to language, for English readers. Similarly, if you only understood Mandarin, the symbol '山' would represent the exact same manifestation in space. So, the goal here is to get comfortable with observing the world without a constant mental description of what it is. Resting in the space of pure witness without the support of language will make you more present. You can use the language to describe from this place of pure perception gradually. It is IMPORTANT to pick a perception from the 3D world and observe

What I mean by "language is not the experience" is that any combination of words we use to express or communicate an experience will not be the same as having that experience itself. Can we speak in a way that is closely and intimately related to the raw perception? Certainly. It is best to start with a perception that is of the physical world or a perception that is sensory in nature.

We can try to describe this sensory perception without any additional perspective that might be personal or biased. We can start by expressing the sounds we hear, the visual perception, or the sensation on our skin. The reason why we have to start with sensory perception right now, in this moment, is that we mostly express opinions about a human being, a situation, or an object in our environment from a biased or judgmental perspective.

We may be aware or unaware of this behavior. So, it is better to pick something in our environment that exists independently of what we think about it. And just start with the raw perception of how it actually feels to have any one of the sensory perceptions. Eventually, we have to get comfortable in simply staying with the experience itself, and get involved with narration consciously if needed.

The only purpose of language is to create a common understanding within a community of what a sound vibration, or when written, a symbol, is supposed to represent of an experience in the perceptual world. If we can clearly understand this and express from this understanding when we communicate, we can avoid a lot of conflicts, miscommunication, and most importantly, we can support the growth of humanity in a direction that is favorable for people, animals, and nature with least resistance.

This environment, in which the communication is very clear, will help the evolution of human consciousness in a more harmonious and livable way. At an individual level, we can make use of this technique of separating language from the experience to initiate the spiritual awakening process. The reason why this can be a way is that the only barrier, or rather the major barrier, why we suffer unnecessarily and delay our awakening is because of the mental narration and beliefs we have set for ourselves of who we are and what the world is. So by temporarily suspending the mental narration, which makes use of language, we can detach ourselves from the belief systems that limit us or restrict our freedom.

One of the key aspects of living an awakened life is the responsible use of language. We see our thoughts before we express them, understanding that language is meant to represent the divine experience of every moment. We also become observant when others speak, intuitively sensing the intention and truthfulness behind their words. This applies not only to human voices, but also to the sounds animals make. We can connect at a deeper level with an animal by sensing the emotion or intention behind its sounds.

Imagine a world without language. This is not merely hypothetical, as we can look back to the early stages of human evolution when people used symbolic carvings on stone to represent events or objects in the world. This is an example of transparent communication. Our task now is to slow down and regularly allocate time to align our language with raw perception. This shift towards a more truthful way of speaking cannot be immediate; it requires time and is a gradual progress.

Improving our language skills is not just about grammar and vocabulary. While it's beneficial to have accurate grammar, it's more important that every word we use reflects the true emotion of the perception we're trying to convey. You can start your day with this practice every morning. Sit in any position you like, not to meditate or exercise, but to observe the world from your current point and see if your perception changes.

Close your eyes to eliminate visual perception, leaving you with sounds and bodily sensations. Start by listening to a sound. For example, you might hear a bird chirping in the morning. You could describe this sound as that of a dog or a bird. In both cases, the quality of the experience doesn't change – the bird continues to chirp. However, describing the sound as that of a bird more accurately represents the form in the world that is producing the sound. This is a simple example of how you can align your language and experience with each of your perceptions.

The best way to spend your time when you're alone or when there's no external noise demanding your response is to stop using language to narrate experiences to yourself. Instead, choose to witness the world as it is, without judging the experiences. It's also vitally important to read and speak responsibly. Don't overindulge in reading; read for the love of reading, not out of compulsion. When you speak, speak from the heart, from the space where you have awakened your body, your language, and your thoughts, which emanate from the space of pure knowing.

Recognizing the One Intelligence

The concept of a singular, universal intelligence that underlies all of existence is a theme that resonates across various philosophical and spiritual traditions. This intelligence is seen as the creative force that gives rise to every form in the universe, from the smallest particle to the vast galaxies. This same intelligence is also us, trying to understand its own creation. We are not separate observers of the universe; we are integral parts of it. Our very existence, our thoughts, emotions, and experiences, are manifestations of this intelligence.

The realization that "We are It" is a profound shift in understanding. It moves us beyond the illusion of separateness and into a state of unity with all of existence. To emphasize again, this is not a conceptual understanding but a deep, intuitive knowing that transcends intellectual knowledge.

This realization does not come as a result of adopting another belief system or drawing conclusions based on limited observations or mental constructs. Instead, it emerges from a state of pure perception, where we see things as they are, free from the filters of our conditioned mind. Pure perception is a state of clear, unfiltered awareness. It is a state where we perceive reality directly, without the interference of our thoughts, beliefs, or preconceived notions. Cultivating this state of pure perception is a key aspect of the journey towards recognizing the one intelligence.

As we cultivate this state of pure perception, the realization that "We are It" becomes more and more apparent. We begin to see the interconnectedness of all things and recognize the one intelligence that underlies all of existence. In the realm of spirituality, there exists a concept of a primary, intuitive understanding, often referred to as the 'First Knowing' or 'Divine Knowing'. This form of knowledge, traditionally called self-knowledge, is considered the foundation of what can be termed 'Common Sense Spirituality'.

The 'First Knowing' is an intuitive understanding that precedes conceptualization or intellectual analysis. It is a direct, immediate awareness that arises from within, independent of sensory input or mental constructs. This knowing is often associated with a sense of clarity, peace, and profound understanding.

In spiritual traditions, this 'First Knowing' is often referred to as 'Divine Knowing'. It is seen as a glimpse into the divine essence of reality, a direct experience of the truth that underlies all existence. This divine knowing is not something that we acquire or learn; it is something that we uncover or remember. It is a part of our inherent nature, often obscured by the noise and distractions of our everyday mind. Self-knowledge, in the spiritual context, refers to the understanding of our true nature. It is the realization that we are not merely physical beings having a temporary human experience, but spiritual beings in essence.

Self-knowledge is often considered the heart of spirituality. It is the cornerstone of spiritual growth and the ultimate goal of many spiritual paths. The journey towards self-knowledge involves introspection, meditation, and mindful living. It is a journey of self-discovery, leading to the realization of our inherent divinity and interconnectedness with all existence.

Common Sense Spirituality refers to a practical, down-to-earth approach to spirituality. It emphasizes direct experience over beliefs, intuition over intellect, and simplicity over complexity. It is about recognizing the sacred in the ordinary, finding wisdom in everyday experiences, and seeing the extraordinary within the ordinary. In Common Sense Spirituality, the 'First Knowing' or 'Divine Knowing' plays a crucial role. It serves as a guiding light, leading us towards self-knowledge and spiritual awakening. It reminds us that spirituality is not about adhering to dogmas or performing rituals, but about awakening to our true nature and living in harmony with it.

Chapter 8

Side Effects: Peace and Fearlessness

"One day I will find the right words, and they will be simple." - Jack Kerouac

---

Spirituality and meditation have gained widespread popularity in recent years, often touted as tools for achieving peace, happiness, and stress relief. While these benefits are indeed aspects of spiritual practices, they are merely the side effects and not the ultimate goal. Unfortunately, many people approach with the sole purpose of chasing these side effects, overlooking the profound depth and transformative potential these practices hold.

In our social media validated, stress-filled modern world, these practices offer a refuge, a way to calm the mind, manage emotions, and cultivate a sense of inner peace. There's no denying that these benefits are valuable and contribute to improving one's quality of life. However, they are not the end goal but rather the by-products of a deeper, transformative process. When people approach spirituality and meditation with the sole aim of achieving peace, happiness, or stress relief, they limit their experience and understanding of these practices. They risk turning these profound practices into mere coping mechanisms or relaxation techniques.

This approach can lead to a form of spiritual materialism, where spiritual practices are used to fulfill personal desires or escape from unpleasant experiences. It can also lead to attachment to the side effects, where one's spiritual practice becomes dependent on experiencing peace, happiness, or relief from stress. Spirituality and meditation hold a much more profound depth than just providing peace, happiness, or stress relief. At their core, these practices are about self-discovery and self-transformation. They are about understanding the nature of the self, the mind, and reality. They are about cultivating awareness, compassion, and wisdom.

Through spirituality and meditation, one can delve into the depths of consciousness, transcend the ego, and experience a sense of oneness with all existence. These practices can lead to the realization of our inherent divinity and interconnectedness, often referred to as self-realization or enlightenment. Perhaps the most significant potential of spirituality and meditation is the discovery of God itself, or the ultimate reality. This is not about believing in a particular concept of God, but about directly experiencing the divine essence that pervades all of existence. It is not about accumulating knowledge or adhering to beliefs, but about transcending the mind and experiencing reality as it is. It is about realizing that we are not separate from God or the universe, but are expressions of the same divine essence.

The essence of Human exploration

Delving into the essence of spirituality involves going beyond the surface-level benefits and exploring the deeper, transformative aspects of spiritual practices. Here are some examples of how we can do this:

Cultivating Awareness: Instead of using meditation merely as a relaxation tool, use it as a practice to cultivate awareness and mindfulness. Pay attention to your thoughts, emotions, and sensations without judgment, and observe how they arise and pass away. This can lead to insights about the impermanent and interconnected nature of existence.

Embracing Uncertainty: Spirituality involves embracing the mystery and uncertainty of life. Instead of seeking comfort and security, learn to be comfortable with not knowing. This openness can lead to a deeper understanding of the nature of life and reality.

Practicing Compassion: Go beyond personal well-being and cultivate compassion for all beings. Practices like loving-kindness meditation can help in developing empathy and understanding, leading to a sense of interconnectedness with all of existence.

Self-Inquiry: Engage in self-inquiry to understand the nature of the self. Ask questions like "Who am I?" and "What is the nature of my existence?" This introspection can lead to self-realization and a deeper understanding of one's true nature.

Living Mindfully: Instead of confining spirituality to specific practices or rituals, incorporate it into everyday life. Practice mindfulness in daily activities and interactions. This can transform ordinary experiences into spiritual ones and lead to a greater sense of presence and engagement with life.

Remember, spirituality is a personal journey, and these are just some ways to delve deeper into it. The path may vary for each individual, but the essence remains the same: to understand the nature of existence and realize our interconnectedness with all of life.

The Confident Presence

In the journey of self-discovery and spiritual growth, we often come across the concept of being a confident presence with a gentle smile, knowing the self in every moment. This state of being is not about the ego that dwells in the past or future, but about recognizing our true nature as an all-pervading presence. The confident presence is a state of being where we are fully present in the moment, aware of our existence, and at peace with ourselves. It is characterized by a gentle smile, symbolizing inner peace, acceptance, and joy. This presence is not dependent on external circumstances or validation, but arises from a deep understanding and acceptance of the self.

This confident presence is not about arrogance or self-importance, which are traits of the ego. Instead, it is about recognizing our inherent worth and divinity, independent of our achievements, failures, or how others perceive us. Knowing the self is a fundamental aspect of spiritual growth. It is about recognizing our true nature beyond the physical body and the thinking mind.

This self-knowing is an all-pervading presence. It is always there, in every moment, underlying all our experiences. It is what remains when we let go of our thoughts, emotions, and sensory perceptions. It is the silent witness, the pure awareness that observes without judgment or preference. The ego, in spiritual terms, is our false sense of identity. It is the 'I' that identifies with our thoughts, emotions, body, and experiences. The ego dwells in the past and future, constantly swinging between memories and anticipations. It is driven by desire and fear, constantly seeking pleasure and avoiding pain.

However, when we cultivate a confident presence and know the self, we transcend the ego. We realize that we are not our thoughts, emotions, or experiences, but the awareness that perceives them. We learn to live in the present moment, free from the pull of the past and the push of the future. As we deepen our practice, we start to recognize the silent witness within us, the pure awareness that is our true nature. We begin to experience ourselves as a confident presence, smiling gently at the play of life.

Hitting the gold mine of fulfillment within, seamlessly

Let's explore this unique mine, a mine of fulfillment that resides within us. This mine is special because it never depletes, no matter how much we mine it. Moreover, you can access this mine seamlessly whenever you wish. It's a simple realization that we are already immersed in an ocean of fulfillment and happiness. This fulfillment can be achieved in any interaction we have; every activity we undertake can be equally satisfying and fulfilling. This is a result of recognizing the non-separation between us, that is, the body-mind complex, and the world.

To access this readily available ocean of happiness, we need to let go of our existing belief that satisfaction can only be derived from external objects or a select set of activities. Just like locating a minefield requires initial research or effort, recognizing this ever-present ocean of fulfillment and bliss in every moment requires some initial effort, to quieten down and simply observe using your attention and curiosity.

In this process, you'll realize that the body-mind complex, which you refer to as 'me', is just another object in that ocean of non-separation or bliss. Numerous scriptures have been written about finding this goldmine within. So, I will attempt to refresh and rejuvenate the method to access this ultimate source of fulfillment within.

We might approach this ocean assuming that we are on land, trying to go against the waves to reach the depth of the ocean. However, this analogy of happiness being the ocean has its limitations. It's not a physical representation. Rather, you have to translate this into a felt experience as you contemplate. The contemplation here is to try to find a separation in the experience you're having right now, a separation between you and the experience.

In order to discover the gold mine of fulfillment within, every moment, you must first temporarily set aside your current understanding of the world and your identity. This discovery is so simple that it may initially shock you, and your ego, which has carried significant weight and momentum for years, may naturally resist this discovery, insisting that it can't be this easy.

You can gradually adjust the mental narrative of who you think you are, both as a character and as a physical body, without resisting the experience of fluctuating sensations. It's true that you have the human body as a tool to experience and interact with the world and play your role in our story.

A key aspect of discovering this gold mine of boundless happiness, the happiness that comes simply from being alive, is laughing at yourself and wondering how you missed this all these years. How did you miss seeing the ultimate reality in every moment, in every object, and in every experience? This astonishing discovery is a result of dispelling the non-existent separation between two things: you and the world, me and life.

From the moment you were born, there were never two separate entities. It was the same singular consciousness, the ultimate intelligence, being born into this world, trying to experience it through each of us. This consciousness extends not just to human forms, but to any biological creature we can find on the planet. As human beings, we have this meta-cognition of recognizing or asking existential questions and finding our way back in time to the timeless again.

We always seek fulfillment, whether in this moment or something we wish to attain in the future. An activity you are doing right now can be a stepping stone you have built for yourself to reach that ultimate fulfillment. However, it's very important to take some time to understand why we have set this ultimate goal or fulfillment. Why do we believe that achieving this will bring us more relief?

In most cases, we would have set this ultimate desire as a result of societal requirements. Of course, the first step in this can be related to the survival of yourself and the family involved in your life. Beyond this, any achievements we make may arise to fulfill your childhood desires or the dream of leading a life of social validation from the outside.

You may have knowingly or unknowingly invested the weight of your identity for the outside world to validate. It's important to imagine, hypothetically, who you would be without the role you are playing right now. The role which is invested in receiving validation from society. I'm not suggesting that you should abandon the role you're playing right now. Rather, I'm referring to the possibility of you performing the same role without seeking validation from society.

Ensuring that the fulfillment you seek from a role doesn't dictate your state of being is crucial. You can further expand in the same role without the fear of rejection from an authority or a person in the field. When you clearly understand that each role is limited and specific to eliciting a particular response during an activity, you see that you are already complete.

You are acting from a place of fulfillment, performing the role for the love of immersing yourself in the non-separation that you intuitively recognize. This is a noble way of performing any activity. You will be less stressed when you are already fulfilled and content within because, you know yourself not from a limited identity perspective, but as a whole in which the role is a subset. So, that will be your starting point, and you will not be seeking fulfillment from those limited activities. Instead, every activity will be an expression from this fulfilled, content space.

Let us all tap into this perpetual and causeless space of fulfillment and happiness. We can all dedicate some time, at least to start, to simply observe this space. This is not a forceful activity, but rather, it should be a loving practice.

Engage in a daily practice to see who you are without the story of your life. This practice allows you to connect with your true self, beyond the narratives and memories that often define us.

You are very much welcome to include the story of your past, your memories, and who you think you are. However, this should be done gradually, after recognizing who you are without the baggage of the story. This process allows for a deeper understanding of self, unencumbered by past narratives.

Truth for Truth's Sake

The pursuit of truth for its own sake is a fundamental aspect of human nature. This innate curiosity, the desire to understand the world around us, has been the driving force behind our evolution as a species. It is this quest for truth that has led us to pose existential questions, to stay curious, and to remain aware of our experiences. We will look into the importance of knowing the truth for truth's sake and how it supports the evolution of humanity towards awakened consciousness.

Truth, in its purest form, is a concept that transcends personal beliefs, cultural norms, and societal constructs. It is an objective reality that exists independently of our perceptions. The pursuit of truth for its own sake is not about personal gain or advantage. It is about understanding the world as it truly is, unfiltered by personal biases or preconceived notions.

This pursuit is not easy. It requires a willingness to question, to doubt, and to challenge our own beliefs. It requires us to be open to new ideas, to be willing to change our minds in the face of new evidence. It requires us to be humble, to acknowledge that we do not have all the answers, and to be willing to learn from others. Human beings are unique in our ability to pose existential questions. We ask questions like "Who am I?", "Where is the world arising from?", "What are the boundaries?" etc. These questions force us to confront the reality of our existence, to grapple with the mysteries of life and death, and to seek answers that go beyond the surface level.

Existential questions push us to explore the depths of our consciousness, to delve into the realms of philosophy, spirituality, and science. They challenge us to look beyond the physical world, to contemplate the nature of reality, and to seek a deeper understanding of our place in the universe. Curiosity and awareness are essential tools in our quest for truth. Curiosity drives us to explore, to learn, and to grow. It pushes us to question the status quo, to seek out new experiences, and to continually expand our understanding of the world.

Awareness, on the other hand, allows us to be in the raw perception and to observe our experiences without judgment. It enables us to recognize the interconnectedness of all things, to see the beauty in the mundane, and to find joy in the simple act of being. The evolution of humanity towards awakened consciousness is a journey of self-discovery, of understanding our true nature, and of realizing our potential as conscious beings. It is about transcendence which acknowledges our physical existence, embracing our spiritual nature, and realizing that we are part of a larger, interconnected whole.

This journey is not a destination, but a continuous process of growth and evolution. It is about becoming more aware, more compassionate, and more in tune with the world around us. It is about realizing that we are not separate from the world, but a part of it, and that our actions have a profound impact on the world and the people around us.

Part 3- Evolution in Awakened Consciousness

Chapter 9

The Gradual Alignment

"Words are but symbols for the relations of things to one another and to us; nowhere do they touch upon the absolute truth." - Friedrich Nietzsche

---

 Manifest, the world or life as we know through the 5 senses

 Unmanifest, that will appear as the world

Our story is a journey, a narrative that unfolds with each passing moment. This journey is often guided and sometimes misled by a dualistic way of living, a perspective that sees the world in terms of opposites: good and bad, right and wrong, us and them. Let us look into the momentum of this life story, the challenges of shifting to a non-dualistic way of living, and the natural state of being that emerges from this shift.

From the moment we are born, we are thrust into a world of dualities. We learn to categorize and differentiate, to judge and evaluate. This dualistic perspective becomes the lens through which we view the world, shaping our thoughts, actions, and experiences. This momentum of a dualistic life story is perpetuated by societal norms, cultural beliefs, personal biases. It is a momentum that can be difficult to break, as it is often deeply ingrained in our psyche.

Shifting to a non-dualistic perspective is not a simple task. It requires a radical reorientation of our worldview, a willingness to let go of deeply held beliefs, and the courage to embrace uncertainty. This shift involves moving beyond the binary oppositions that dominate our thinking, to a perspective that sees the interconnectedness and interdependence of all things. It involves recognizing that the distinctions we make between self and other, between inner and outer, are ultimately artificial constructs.

Non-dualism is often described as the natural state of being, a state of consciousness that transcends the dualities of the phenomenal world. In this state, there is no separation between subject and object, no distinction between self and other. There is only pure awareness, a state of oneness with all that is. This state of non-dual consciousness is not something that can be achieved or attained. It is not a destination, but rather a realization of what has always been present. It is a recognition of our true nature, a return to our original state of wholeness and unity.

The movement from dualism to non-dualism is a transformative process, a shift in consciousness that has the potential to radically alter our experience of the world. It is a journey that requires patience, perseverance, and a willingness to question the assumptions that underpin our dualistic worldview. While this journey can be challenging, it is also profoundly liberating. As we let go of our dualistic tendencies, we open ourselves to a new way of being, a state of non-dual consciousness that is our natural state of being. In this state, we are free from the constraints of dualistic thinking, able to experience the world in all its richness and complexity. We are, in essence, returning home to ourselves.

Starting with Body movement

The practice of daily contemplation and meditation can serve as a powerful tool to reconnect with our natural state and initiate self-healing. The next bit will look into the importance of planning formal contemplation and meditation sessions every day to observe the body and the world around us.

Planning formal contemplation and meditation sessions every day is crucial for several reasons. Firstly, it helps to establish a routine, making it easier to incorporate these practices into our daily lives. Secondly, it ensures that we dedicate a specific time each day to self-reflection and self-care, which is often neglected in our busy schedules. These sessions don't have to be lengthy; even a few minutes each day can make a significant difference. The key is consistency. Over time, these daily practices can become a natural part of our lives, just like eating or sleeping.

One of the fundamental aspects of contemplation and meditation is the practice of observation. This involves paying attention to our physical sensations, thoughts, and emotions, as well as the world around us. By observing our bodies, we can become more aware of our physical health and well-being, noticing any signs of stress or tension. Observing the world around us, on the other hand, can help us to cultivate a sense of connection and interdependence. It allows us to appreciate the beauty and complexity of the natural world, fostering the sense of awe and wonder.

There is a state of presence, awareness, and acceptance, free from the constraints of the ego and the incessant chatter of the mind. In this state, we can experience a sense of peace, joy, and contentment that is independent of external circumstances. Contemplation and meditation also have the potential to initiate self-healing. By reducing stress, improving mental clarity, and promoting emotional balance, these practices can enhance our overall health and well-being. They can help us to heal from past traumas, cope with present challenges, and cultivate resilience for the future.

The human body is a marvel of nature that serves as the vessel for our consciousness. However, in our day-to-day lives, we often overlook the importance of body awareness and the role it plays in our overall well-being. A part of gradual shift is in increasing body awareness, loosening the mental identity with the body, and allowing the intelligence of our consciousness to move and relax into the aware space.

Body awareness refers to the ability to pay attention to our bodies, to recognize and understand the signals it sends us. This includes being aware of our physical sensations, our movements, and our posture. Increasing body awareness can have profound effects on both our physical and mental health.

By becoming more attuned to our bodies, we can better understand our needs, our limitations, and our potential. We can learn to listen to our bodies, to respect its signals, and to respond appropriately. This can lead to improved physical health, reduced stress, and increased self-confidence. Our mental identity with the body is often deeply ingrained. We tend to view our bodies as a solid part of who we are, a fixed and unchangeable aspect of our identity. However, this perspective can limit our understanding of ourselves and our potential.

By loosening our mental identity with the body, we can begin to see ourselves in a new light. We can recognize that our bodies are not fixed or static, but dynamic and ever-changing. We can understand that our bodies are not separate from the world around us, but intimately connected to it. Our consciousness is not confined to our minds, but permeates our entire being. It is the intelligence that guides our thoughts, our emotions, and our actions. By allowing the intelligence of our consciousness to move and relax into the aware space, we can tap into this innate wisdom.

This involves letting go of our preconceived notions, our judgments, and our fears. It involves opening ourselves up to the present moment, to the richness of our experiences, and to the depth of our being. It involves embracing the uncertainty, the mystery, and the beauty of life.

Mental Space and Sensory experience of world

Awakening to our natural state of consciousness is a transformative journey that involves a profound shift in our understanding and experience of the world. This journey often leads to a clearer perception of our mental space and sensory experiences, allowing us to live more fully and authentically. Our natural state of consciousness is often described as a state of pure awareness, free from the distortions of the mind and the limitations of the senses. In this state, we are fully present and engaged with the world around us, yet we remain detached from the transient thoughts and emotions that often cloud our perception.

This state of consciousness is not something that we need to attain or achieve. Rather, it is our inherent nature, always available to us beneath the layers of conditioning and habitual patterns of thought and behavior. Awakening to this natural state involves peeling away these layers to reveal the pure awareness that lies beneath.

Mental space, or the mind's capacity for awareness, plays a crucial role in this process of awakening. As we cultivate mindfulness and develop the ability to observe our thoughts and emotions without judgment, we begin to create space in our minds. This mental space allows us to see our experiences more clearly, without the filter of our conditioned responses.

In this expanded mental space, we can observe the rise and fall of thoughts and emotions, recognizing them as transient phenomena that do not define us. We can also see the patterns and habits that have shaped our responses to the world, and choose to respond in more conscious and intentional ways. Awakening to our natural state of consciousness also transforms our sensory experience of the world. Freed from the constraints of the mind, our senses become more acute, allowing us to experience the world in a more direct and immediate way.

Sounds, sights, tastes, smells, and tactile sensations become richer and more nuanced. We may find that we are able to appreciate the beauty and complexity of the world around us in ways that we never have before. This heightened sensory awareness can bring a sense of wonder and awe, and a deep appreciation for the miracle of existence.

Continuous process towards collective awakening

The evolution of human consciousness is a fascinating journey, marked by a gradual awakening at the collective level. This awakening is not just about individual enlightenment, but also about our collective growth as a species. As we navigate this journey, compassion towards the unwillingly ignorant and self-compassion become essential tools for fostering understanding and promoting spiritual growth. Humanity's gradual awakening can be seen as a shift from a state of unconsciousness, where actions are driven by instinct and conditioning, to a state of conscious awareness, where actions are guided by insight and understanding. This shift is not a sudden event, but a gradual process that unfolds over time.

This awakening is happening at the collective level, as we, as a species, are beginning to recognize our interconnectedness and the impact of our actions on the world around us. We are starting to see that our well-being is intimately connected with the well-being of others and the planet. As we awaken, we inevitably encounter those who remain unaware or unwillingly ignorant of this interconnected reality. It's easy to feel frustrated or impatient with those who seem stuck in old patterns of thought and behavior. However, it's important to remember that we all are at different stages of our own awakening process.

Compassion towards the unwillingly ignorant is not about condoning harmful behavior or ignoring injustice. Rather, it's about recognizing the ignorance as a lack of awareness and understanding. It's about responding with patience, kindness, and a genuine desire to help foster understanding.

Just as we need compassion for others, we also need self-compassion. Awakening is not a linear process, and there will be times when we stumble or lose our way. In these moments, self-compassion allows us to meet our shortcomings with understanding and kindness, rather than judgment or criticism. Self-compassion also involves recognizing that our mistakes and failures are part of the shared human experience. This recognition can help us to feel more connected with others, even in our moments of struggle. As we cultivate compassion and self-compassion, we open ourselves up to deeper insights into the true nature of spirituality. Spirituality, in its essence, is about recognizing our interconnectedness and cultivating qualities like love, compassion, and understanding.

These insights do not come all at once, but gradually, as we continue to practice and deepen our understanding. Each insight brings us closer to our true nature and helps us to live more authentically and fully.

Thoughts and Awakening

Thoughts are an integral part of our consciousness. They arise from our experiences, beliefs, and perceptions, forming a continuous narrative that shapes our reality. However, it's important to understand that these thoughts often arise on behalf of a self that still sees the world through the filter of a separate self. This separate self, or ego, is a construct of our minds, formed through our unique experiences and societal conditioning.

When we identify with this ego, our thoughts are colored by its perceptions and biases. These thoughts can often lead to feelings of separation, fear, and anxiety. However, by recognizing that these thoughts are arising on behalf of the ego, we can begin to disidentify from them and see them for what they truly are - just thoughts. As we gradually investigate our thoughts, we can begin to explore how they would be if they were representing our identity of presence, rather than our ego. The identity of presence refers to our true self, the pure consciousness that exists beyond the ego. This is the part of us that is connected to all things, that is in the present moment, and that is free from judgment and fear. When our thoughts represent this identity of presence, they are not colored by the ego's biases or fears. Instead, they arise from a place of love, acceptance, and unity. They allow us to see the world as it truly is, without the filter of the separate self.

The process of awakening involves eliminating unnecessary thoughts that rob us from being and experiencing the world with active perception. These are the thoughts that arise from the ego, that keep us trapped in cycles of fear, judgment, and separation. By recognizing these thoughts for what they are, we can choose not to engage with them. We can allow them to arise and pass, without identifying with them or allowing them to pull us out of the present moment. This allows us to stay rooted in our identity of presence.

Language is a powerful tool that allows us to express our thoughts, feelings, and experiences. It is a representation of our experience in the physical world, a medium through which we communicate and understand our reality. However, our perception of this reality can often be biased by our thought processes, ideas, and past experiences. Language is intrinsically linked to our physical experiences. The words we use are often metaphors for the physical world around us. For instance, we use words like "warm" or "cold" to describe not just physical temperatures, but also emotions and relationships. In this way, language serves as a bridge between our internal subjective experiences and the external objective world.

However, language is not just a passive reflection of reality. It actively shapes our perception of the world. The words we choose to describe our experiences can influence how we interpret and remember those experiences. This is known as the linguistic relativity hypothesis, or the Sapir-Whorf hypothesis, which suggests that our thoughts and behaviors are influenced by the language we speak.

While language allows us to articulate our experiences, it can also limit our perception of reality. We are often lost in our thought processes, entangled in our own ideas and imaginations based on past experiences. These thoughts and ideas can create a filter through which we perceive the world, leading to a biased experience of reality.

For example, if we have had negative experiences in the past, we might view the world through a lens of fear or pessimism. Conversely, positive experiences might lead us to perceive the world with optimism. This bias can color our interpretation of events, our interactions with others, and even our understanding of ourselves. To experience reality without the bias of our thoughts and perceptions, we must learn to observe our thoughts without judgment or resistance. This involves recognizing that our thoughts are just that - thoughts. They are not reality itself, but interpretations of reality.

By observing our thoughts, we can begin to see the patterns and biases that shape our perception of the world. We can notice how our past experiences influence our current thought processes and learn to let go of these biases. This process of self-awareness and introspection is often referred to as awakening.

Chapter 10

Appearance Continues

"The most important things are the hardest to say, because words diminish them." - Stephen King

---

Stories of saints and sages, filled with tales of mystical experiences and divine revelations, often shape our expectations of what awakening should be like. We tend to visualize a subjective experience, imagining fireworks, instant enlightenment, or a sudden transformation. However, these expectations can become one of the biggest obstacles in the path to awakening.

Expectations are projections of our desires and fears. They are based on our past experiences, beliefs, and conditioning. When we expect a certain outcome, we create a mental image of what that outcome should be like. This image can limit our perception and prevent us from experiencing the present moment as it is.

Mystical experiences, while profound and transformative, are often temporary. They can provide glimpses into the divine, but they are not the end goal of the spiritual journey. The true essence of awakening lies not in these fleeting experiences, but in the continuous recognition of the divine in the everyday world. Chasing after mystical experiences can lead to a spiritual bypass, where we use spirituality to avoid dealing with our unresolved emotional issues, traumas, and psychological wounds. This can result in a superficial form of spirituality, where we become more focused on achieving certain states of consciousness rather than on the process of self-discovery and transformation. The intention in the path to awakening should always be to see the divine in the physical world under sober circumstances. This means recognizing the sacredness in the ordinary, the extraordinary in the mundane. It involves seeing the world not as separate from the divine, but as a manifestation of it.

This perspective shifts the focus from seeking external validation or experiences to cultivating an inner sense of peace and contentment. It encourages us to embrace the world as it is, without judgment or resistance. This acceptance allows us to experience the world more fully, without the filter of our expectations or imaginations.

The Quality of Experience

The journey from identifying with the ego to recognizing oneself as consciousness is a process that significantly alters our perception of the world. This shift in identity not only changes how we view ourselves but also enhances the quality of our experiences. Let's explores how this transition leads to a more detailed, fearless, and non-judgmental perception of the world.

The ego is our constructed self-identity, formed through our personal experiences, societal conditioning, and the roles we play. It is often associated with our physical existence and is subject to emotions, desires, fears, and judgments.

Consciousness, on the other hand, is our true self, the pure awareness that observes without judgment. It is the silent witness to our experiences, unaffected by the transient emotions or thoughts that pass through our minds. When we shift our identity from the ego to consciousness, our perception of the world undergoes a profound transformation. We begin to see the world not through the lens of our personal biases and judgments, but as it truly is.

As consciousness, we become more present and attentive to our surroundings. Our minds are no longer preoccupied with past regrets or future anxieties, allowing us to fully engage with the present moment. This heightened attention enables us to perceive more details in our environment, enhancing the richness of our experiences. Identifying as consciousness also liberates us from fear. The ego, being attached to its identity and survival, is often dominated by fear. However, consciousness, being eternal and unchanging, is free from such fears. This allows us to observe the world fearlessly, embracing all experiences with equanimity.

The shift to consciousness also cultivates patience. As we disidentify from the ego, we let go of our desires for instant gratification. We become more patient, allowing experiences to unfold naturally without rushing or forcing outcomes.

Finally, recognizing ourselves as consciousness fosters a non-judgmental perception. The ego tends to categorize experiences as good or bad based on its preferences. Consciousness, however, perceives without judgment, accepting all experiences as part of the diverse tapestry of life.

The story will continue

A profound realization of our true nature beyond the ego, is often seen as an end point, a destination where our story concludes. However, awakening is not the end of our journey, but rather a transformation that allows us to engage with the world in a more authentic and meaningful way. A bit on how our story and role continue even after awakening, and how we can choose to engage with the world and society.

Awakening does not erase our past or the roles we play in the world. We still have a story, a narrative that is woven from our experiences, relationships, and interactions. This story continues to unfold even after awakening, but it is no longer the defining aspect of our identity. Instead, it becomes a part of the rich tapestry of our existence, a unique expression of the consciousness that we are.

Our roles in the world also continue after awakening. We may still be parents, children, friends, professionals, artists, or activists. However, these roles no longer confine or define us. They are simply aspects of our experience, ways in which we engage with the world. After awakening, we may choose to engage with the world we knew, the relationships we had, and the roles we played. However, this engagement is likely to be different. It is no longer driven by the ego's desires or fears, but by a deeper sense of purpose and connection.

We may find that our relationships become more authentic and meaningful. We are able to relate to others not as separate entities, but as expressions of the same consciousness. This shift in perception can bring about a deeper sense of empathy and compassion, transforming our interactions and relationships. Awakening also opens up the possibility of contributing to society in a more meaningful way. If there is a social issue that concerns us, we can choose to get involved and work towards a resolution. This is not a compulsion, but a choice that arises from a deep sense of connection and responsibility towards the world.

Our contribution can take many forms. It could be as simple as being kinder and more compassionate in our daily interactions, or as complex as initiating social change. Regardless of the form it takes, our contribution is likely to be more effective because it is driven by a clear understanding of the interconnectedness of all life.

Navigating Societal Momentum

Societal momentum refers to the prevailing trends, beliefs, and attitudes within a society. It is shaped by historical events, cultural norms, and collective experiences, and it exerts a powerful influence on individual behavior and perception. Even after self-realization, we must navigate this societal momentum, which can often be characterized by ignorance, bias, and rigid beliefs.

This momentum is particularly evident in areas such as politics, nationality, and religion, where strongly held beliefs often lead to division and conflict. These beliefs are typically rooted in the ego, which seeks to assert its identity and superiority over others. The ego war is a metaphor for the struggle for dominance and validation that often characterizes societal interactions. It is a war of "who wins the best right part of the society," where different groups vie for recognition, power, and resources. This ego war is fueled by ignorance and bias, and it often obscures the essence of who we are non-egoically.

In the ego war, the focus is on differences rather than commonalities, on division rather than unity. This perspective can lead to a narrow understanding of the world, where the value of individuals or groups is determined by their adherence to certain beliefs or their possession of certain attributes.

After self-realization, our perspective shifts from the ego to the consciousness. We recognize that our true nature is not confined to our individual identities or societal roles, but is part of a larger, interconnected whole. This realization can lead to a more compassionate and inclusive perspective, where we see beyond societal divisions and acknowledge the inherent worth of all beings. However, even with this expanded perspective, we still have to navigate the societal momentum. We may face resistance or misunderstanding from those who are still operating from an egoic perspective. It is important to approach these challenges with patience and understanding, recognizing that everyone is at a different point in their journey.

Despite these challenges, self-realization does not necessitate withdrawal from society. On the contrary, it can inspire us to engage more deeply with the world, to contribute to positive change and help alleviate suffering. With our expanded perspective, we can bring a new level of consciousness to our interactions, promoting understanding, empathy, and unity.

Whether it's through participating in political discourse, contributing to community initiatives, or simply practicing kindness in our daily interactions, we can help shift the societal momentum towards greater awareness and inclusivity.

The Long Game of Collective Awakening

The journey of awakening is often perceived as a personal endeavor, a solitary path towards self-realization. However, the process of awakening extends beyond the individual, encompassing the collective consciousness of humanity. It is a long-term game, spanning multiple generations on Earth, lifetimes of reincarnations, and multidimensional influences.

Collective awakening refers to the shared realization of our true nature as conscious beings, transcending the limitations of individual identities and societal constructs. It is a long-term game, requiring patience, perseverance, and a commitment to the greater good.

The process of collective awakening is not confined to a single lifetime or generation. It unfolds over multiple generations, each contributing to the evolution of human consciousness. Every generation has the potential to advance the collective awakening, building on the wisdom and experiences of those who came before them. The concept of reincarnation suggests that our souls undergo multiple lifetimes, each offering unique experiences and lessons. These lifetimes provide opportunities for growth and evolution, contributing to our individual and collective awakening.

In addition to reincarnation, multidimensional influences also play a role in the collective awakening. These influences can come from higher dimensions of consciousness, guiding and supporting our journey towards awakening. They serve as reminders of our true nature, helping us to transcend the ignorance and illusions of the physical world. The current state of humanity is characterized by a high degree of ignorance, with many people identified with their egos and trapped in cycles of fear, greed, and separation. This ignorance is a major obstacle to the collective awakening.

However, through the process of non-egoic self-discovery, we can begin to wash away this ignorance. As we awaken to our true nature, we realize the interconnectedness of all life and the illusion of separation dissolves. We begin to see the world with new eyes, recognizing the divine in all beings and in ourselves.

This shift in perception has the potential to transform society, leading to more compassion, understanding, and unity. It can help to resolve conflicts, heal divisions, and create a more peaceful and harmonious world.

Contributing to the collective awakening can take many forms. Here are some ways you might consider:

Personal Growth: The first step towards contributing to the collective awakening is to focus on your own personal growth and self-realization. This involves cultivating self-awareness, mindfulness, and compassion. As you awaken to your true nature, you naturally contribute to the collective awakening by raising the overall level of consciousness.

Education and Sharing: Share your knowledge, insights, and experiences with others. This could be through writing, speaking, teaching, or simply through your day-to-day interactions with others. By sharing your journey, you can inspire others to embark on their own path of self-discovery.

Service and Activism: Engage in activities that promote the well-being of all beings. This could be through volunteering, activism, or any form of service that aligns with your skills and passions. By working to alleviate suffering and promote justice, equality, and sustainability, you contribute to creating a more conscious and awakened society.

Mindful Relationships: Practice mindfulness and compassion in your relationships. See others not as separate from you, but as reflections of the same consciousness. Do not go into a relationship to transact in happiness, it is not a currency., be the source of happiness in a relationship and do not expect anything in return. This shift in perception can transform your relationships and create a ripple effect that contributes to the collective awakening.

Meditation and Spiritual Practices: Regular meditation or other spiritual practices can help to quiet the mind and open the heart, allowing you to connect more deeply with your true nature. These practices can also have a positive impact on those around you, contributing to the collective awakening.

Remember, every step you take on your personal journey of awakening can contribute to the collective awakening. It's a process that requires patience, compassion, and the understanding that we are all interconnected in this journey.

Temporary Detachment and Patience

We have to discuss the importance of having the courage to detach from the current narrative of humanity, witnessing the chaos from a neutral position, and operating from a space of infinite wisdom. The story of humanity is a tapestry woven from countless individual narratives, societal structures, and historical events. While this story shapes our collective identity and experience, it can also limit our perception and understanding of reality.

Detaching from this story requires courage. It involves stepping back from our ingrained beliefs, biases, and assumptions to observe the world from a neutral position. This doesn't mean rejecting or negating the story of humanity, but rather viewing it as a single perspective among many.

Detachment allows us to witness the chaos, conflicts, and contradictions of our world without being overwhelmed by them. It provides a space for reflection and introspection, enabling us to see beyond the surface-level chaos to the underlying patterns and structures. The process of collective awakening is not an overnight transformation. It's a long-term game that requires patience, perseverance, and a long-term perspective. We must be willing to sit with the discomfort, uncertainty, and ambiguity that often accompany this process.

A long-term perspective allows us to see beyond the immediate challenges and setbacks to the larger trajectory of transformation. It reminds us that every step, no matter how small, contributes to the collective awakening. At the heart of the awakening process is the recognition of our ability to observe. This is the space from which all forms arise, the fundamental reality of the universe. It is the source of all creativity, innovation, and evolution.

Moving and living from this space of infinite potential means recognizing our inherent capacity to create, transform, and evolve. It means seeing ourselves not as fixed entities, but as dynamic, evolving expressions of consciousness.

Chapter 11

Intelligence in Awakened Space

"Silence is the language of God, all else is poor translation." - Rumi

---

Intelligence, in its quest to understand the world, life situations, and survival skills, often operates through the lens of the ego. The ego, with its limited beliefs and perceptions, can restrict the scope of intelligence, confining it to a narrow understanding of reality. However, this intelligence has the potential to transcend these limitations and return to its raw, intuitive, and primordial knowing space.

The ego is a construct of the mind that forms our sense of self. It is shaped by our personal experiences, societal conditioning, and survival instincts. The ego helps us navigate the world, make sense of our experiences, and interact with others. However, the ego also has its limitations. The ego operates based on limited beliefs and perceptions. It views the world through the lens of duality, perceiving things as separate and distinct. This perspective can lead to a fragmented understanding of reality, where we see ourselves as separate from the world and others.

Intelligence, in its purest form, is the ability to understand, learn, and adapt. It is a fundamental aspect of consciousness, enabling us to interact with the world and make sense of our experiences.

However, when intelligence operates through the ego, it becomes confined by the ego's limited beliefs and perceptions. It becomes focused on survival and competition, often overlooking the interconnectedness and interdependence of all life. The first knowing space refers to the raw, intuitive, and primordial state of intelligence. It is the space of pure awareness, free from the constraints of the ego. In this space, intelligence operates based on intuition and direct perception, rather than limited beliefs or assumptions.

Reconnecting with this primal state of awareness necessitates surpassing the constraints of the ego. This calls for the release of our inflexible convictions and viewpoints, thereby exposing ourselves to the immense and intricate nature of existence. This progression isn't about dismissing or denying the ego, but rather about broadening our viewpoint to encompass more than merely the ego. The yearning for a personal experience, when guided by unawareness, leads to the creation of a narrative known as ego identity.

The journey from the ego to the first knowing space is a transformative process. It involves a shift in our understanding of ourselves and the world. As we let go of our limited beliefs and perceptions, we begin to see the world in a new light. We recognize the interconnectedness of all things and the inherent wisdom of nature.

This transformation is not always easy. It requires courage, patience, and perseverance. However, the rewards are immense. As we return to our first knowing space, we experience a sense of peace, clarity, and connection that transcends the limitations of the ego.

The Aware Pure Knowing

Intelligence is often associated with cognitive abilities such as problem-solving, reasoning, and learning. However, from a broader perspective, intelligence can be seen as an aware, pure knowing that transcends cognitive functions. This form of intelligence has the ability to perceive the phenomenal world from a discovered dimension of space and seeks to express and find itself through various activities and experiences.

At its core, intelligence is an aware, pure knowing. It is the fundamental consciousness that underlies all experiences and phenomena. This form of intelligence is not confined to the mind or the cognitive processes; it permeates every aspect of our being, allowing us to perceive and interact with the world.

This pure knowing is not dependent on external information or sensory input. It is an innate awareness, a direct knowing that arises from within. It is this intelligence that allows us to perceive the phenomenal world, not just through our senses, but from a deeper, more holistic perspective.

The phenomenal world refers to the world as we perceive it through our senses. It is the world of forms, colors, sounds, textures, and sensations. However, this is just one dimension of reality.

Beyond the phenomenal world lies the discovered dimension of space. This is the realm of pure consciousness, the source from which all phenomena arise. It is a dimension that is not bound by time, space, or causality. From this dimension, the phenomenal world is seen as a play of forms and phenomena, arising and dissolving in the vast expanse of consciousness.

Intelligence, as pure knowing, seeks to express and find itself in the phenomenal world. It does this through various activities and experiences, each offering an opportunity for expression and discovery. However, these activities and experiences are often pursued with limited agendas, driven by the ego's desires and fears. These limited agendas can restrict the expression of intelligence, confining it to narrow patterns of behavior and perception.

Despite these limitations, intelligence continues to seek satisfaction and fulfillment. It strives to express itself fully, to know itself deeply, and to realize its infinite potential. This striving is not a struggle or a battle, but a natural unfolding, a blossoming of intelligence in its full glory.

Inner Peace and Objective Understanding

In the grand theater of life, each of us plays a unique role. Yet, amidst the drama of existence, it is easy to lose sight of our true selves. Let us explore how understanding oneself as a free witness can help us relax our attention back to the source of creation, view the drama of humanity more objectively, prioritize inner peace, and cultivate an intelligence to survive without greed.

The concept of the 'free witness' refers to the part of us that observes our experiences without judgment or attachment. This observer is always free, unbound by the constraints of time, space, or circumstance. It is the silent watcher of our thoughts, emotions, and actions.

Knowing oneself as this free witness is a profound realization. It means recognizing that we are not merely the sum of our experiences, but the conscious awareness that perceives them. This awareness is always present, always free, and always at peace. It is the source from which all creation springs and to which all creation returns.

When we identify with the free witness within, we can relax our attention back to the source of creation. Instead of getting caught up in the drama of life, we can observe it from a place of detached awareness. This doesn't mean we become passive or indifferent. Rather, it allows us to engage with life more fully, without being overwhelmed by it.

Relaxing our attention back to the source is like tuning into a radio station. When we tune into the frequency of the free witness, we align ourselves with the source of creation. We become attuned to the underlying harmony of the universe, and this alignment brings a sense of peace and clarity. From the perspective of the free witness, we can view the drama of humanity in a more objective way. We can see the interplay of forces that shape human behavior - the desires, fears, and aspirations that drive the drama of life.

This objective view doesn't diminish the significance of human experience. Instead, it enriches it. It allows us to see the beauty and tragedy, the comedy and chaos, the triumphs and trials of human life with a clear, compassionate gaze. Recognizing the free witness within helps us prioritize inner peace. This peace is not dependent on external circumstances. It is a deep, abiding peace that exists at the core of our being.

Prioritizing this inner peace means making choices that align with our true nature. It means letting go of attachments that disturb our peace. It means cultivating attitudes and behaviors that foster peace - such as kindness, compassion, and understanding. The free witness within us knows that we are part of a vast, interconnected web of life. It understands that our survival depends not on greed, but on cooperation and mutual respect.

Surviving without greed requires a shift in perspective. It requires us to see ourselves not as separate, competing entities, but as integral parts of a larger whole. It requires us to trust in the abundance of the universe and to share that abundance with others.

Finally, knowing oneself as the free witness cultivates a trust in all stakeholders, known and unknown. It recognizes that we are all players in the drama of life, each with our own role to play. It trusts in the wisdom of the universe, knowing that each event, each interaction, has its place in the grand scheme of things.

Embracing Infinity

At the core of our being, we are infinite. This is not a concept or a belief, but a fundamental truth of our existence. We are not finite beings having a temporary human experience; rather, we are infinite consciousness experiencing itself through the lens of humanity.

Recognizing our infinite nature means acknowledging that we are more than our physical bodies, more than our thoughts, emotions, and experiences. We are a form of infinity, timeless and boundless, and this has always been the case. The divine presence, or God, that we have been searching for is not an external entity residing in some distant heaven. It is the very essence of our being, the life force that animates us, the consciousness that perceives and experiences reality. It is always here, always available, ever-present in every moment.

This realization is not a mental understanding that can be grasped by the intellect. It is a living reality, an experiential truth that can only be known through direct experience. The ego, with its false identity and ignorance of our true nature, often directs our intelligence. It creates a sense of separation, a belief in scarcity, and a need for competition and control. It keeps us trapped in patterns of fear, desire, and suffering.

When we recognize our infinite nature and the ever-present divine, we can begin to transcend the ego. We can see through its illusions and free ourselves from its grip. We can stop employing our intelligence in the service of the ego and start using it in the service of truth and love.

When our intelligence operates from a place of freedom, wakefulness, and divinity, it becomes a powerful tool for enlightenment. It becomes a means of exploring reality, understanding ourselves, and expressing our unique gifts. This enlightened intelligence is not swayed by the hollow beliefs of the unknown. It does not cling to dogmas or doctrines, but seeks direct experience. It is open, curious, and humble. It questions, investigates, and learns. It is guided by wisdom, compassion, and a deep respect for all life.

Unconscious Neurosis

Unconscious neurosis refers to the mental and emotional patterns that we unknowingly repeat, often leading to stress, anxiety, and dissatisfaction. These patterns can become so ingrained that we accept them as normal, even when they cause us harm.

The biggest service an individual can do for themselves and the world is to recognize and stop this unconscious neurosis. This requires a willingness to look inward, to observe our thoughts and emotions without judgment, and to question the beliefs and assumptions that drive our behavior. Our minds are often filled with a constant stream of thoughts, worries, plans, and memories. This mental chaos can be overwhelming, yet we have become so accustomed to it that we often don't even notice it.

Acknowledging this mental chaos is the first step towards overcoming it. By bringing awareness to our thoughts, we can begin to see them for what they are: transient mental events, not absolute truths. We can learn to observe our thoughts without getting caught up in them, and in doing so, we can find a sense of calm amidst the chaos.

Despite the mental chaos, there are moments of peace to be found. These moments often occur when we are fully present, when our attention is absorbed in the beauty of the natural world.

Nature has a way of quieting the mind. The rustling of leaves, the chirping of birds, the gentle flow of a river - these experiences can draw our attention away from our thoughts and into the present moment. In these moments, we can experience a sense of peace that is free from thought and ego. The journey towards inner peace is not about suppressing or avoiding our thoughts and emotions. It is about learning to observe them with kindness and curiosity, without getting lost in them.

This journey requires patience and perseverance. It involves cultivating mindfulness, the ability to pay attention to the present moment without judgment. It involves learning to respond to our experiences with compassion and understanding, rather than reacting out of habit or fear.

The Practice of Stillness

Stillness is not just another task on our to-do list. It is a journey into the depths of our being, a journey that takes us beyond the realm of the mind. In this state of stillness, we are not thinking, analyzing, or problem-solving. We are simply being. We are observing, witnessing, and experiencing the present moment in its purest form.

Non-dual contemplation is a key aspect of the practice of stillness. It involves observing our experiences without judgment or separation, recognizing the interconnectedness of all things. In this state of contemplation, we are not caught up in the duality of right and wrong, good and bad, self and other. We are simply present, aware, and open to the unfolding of each moment.

The insights gained during non-dual contemplation can have a profound impact on the rest of our activities. When we practice stillness, we cultivate a sense of inner peace and clarity that permeates all aspects of our lives. We become more present, more attuned to our experiences, and more capable of responding to life's challenges with wisdom and compassion.

This heightened awareness can enhance the quality of our involvement in other activities. Whether we are working, studying, exercising, or interacting with others, we can bring the same presence and openness that we cultivate in stillness. In this way, stillness can enrich our lives, not just during the practice itself, but in every moment.

Beyond Beliefs and Dualities

The divine, often conceptualized as a supreme power or universal consciousness, is a subject of contemplation across various cultures and religions. However, the divine is not confined to our thoughts, beliefs, or religious doctrines. It is an ever-present reality, pure and innocent, always eager to discover itself amidst the imagined limitations of human existence. Without getting mystical, let us see how we can witness the divine right now and the implications of this realization on our understanding of reality.

The Truth does not care about our thoughts or what we think about its nature. It remains unaffected by our beliefs, religious doctrines, or scientific theories. It is always pure, always innocent, and always present. It does not require our belief to exist, nor does it cease to exist in the face of disbelief. It is not an object of thought, but the subject of experience. It is not something we think about, but something we witness, something we experience directly. It is not a concept, but a living reality.

We can witness the capital 'T' Truth right now, in this very moment. It is not a distant reality to be sought or attained, but the very essence of our being, the life force that animates us, the consciousness that perceives and experiences reality.

Witnessing the highest involves shifting our attention from the realm of thoughts to the realm of direct experience. It involves quieting the mind and tuning into the subtle vibrations of life. It involves opening our hearts to the mystery of existence and surrendering to the flow of life.

The divine is always eager to discover itself, even when shrouded in the imagined limitations of human existence.

These limitations, whether they be physical, mental, or emotional, are not obstacles to the divine, but opportunities for its expression.

The infinity expresses itself through the diversity of life, through the myriad forms and phenomena of the universe. It expresses itself through the challenges and triumphs of human existence, through the joys and sorrows, the hopes and fears, the love and longing of the human heart. Our dualistic scientific endeavor, with its focus on objective observation and empirical evidence, often seems at odds with the non-dual nature of the divine. However, science and spirituality are not mutually exclusive, but complementary paths to truth.

Science embarks on a journey to investigate the external world, the realm of tangible entities and observable events. It aims to decipher the principles that rule the physical cosmos and the mechanisms that mold life and matter. Conversely, spirituality delves into the internal world, the sphere of consciousness and personal experiences. It strives to comprehend the essence of the individual, the origin of perception and existence. This doesn't imply that the discovered laws are negated or dismissed. Indeed, the possibility to broaden our grasp of the physical laws amplifies when we incorporate the aspect of consciousness into our research. For example, Quantum physics has introduced concepts such as superposition (the idea that a particle can exist in multiple states at once) and entanglement (the phenomenon where particles become interconnected and the state of one can instantly affect the state of the other, regardless of the distance between them). These concepts, while scientifically grounded, have parallels in spiritual philosophies.

For instance, the principle of superposition resonates with spiritual teachings about the nature of reality and perception. Many spiritual traditions suggest that reality is not fixed but is shaped by our perceptions, similar to how a particle in superposition doesn't settle into a definite state until it's observed.

Similarly, the phenomenon of entanglement echoes spiritual teachings about the interconnectedness of all things. Many spiritual philosophies propose that everything in the universe is interconnected and that we are all part of a larger whole, much like the interconnected particles in quantum entanglement.

In this way, science and spirituality can complement each other. Science provides a rigorous, empirical approach to understanding the universe, while spirituality offers a framework for interpreting these findings in the context of our personal experiences and inner lives. Together, they can offer a more holistic understanding of reality. It's important to note, however, that while they can complement each other, science and spirituality represent different approaches to understanding the world, each with its own methodologies and criteria for truth.

Formal and Informal Practices

Formal

The following recommended practices should be carried out consistently. You can choose one or more of these practices and engage with them out of a desire to understand the essence of experience in its purest perception, devoid of mental commentary. One key point to bear in mind during these formal sessions is not to adopt the persona of a meditator or seeker at the outset. Simply initiate the process with an inquisitive curious mind and, as highlighted in the chapters, pursue the Truth for the sake of Truth itself.

Body Scan:

This brief body scan meditation, lasting between five to ten minutes, can be performed before bedtime or at any time during the day to help you reconnect with your body:

- Find a comfortable position, either sitting or lying down, and take five deep, slow breaths. Pay attention to the physical sensation of each breath as it enters and exits your body.
- During one complete breath, focus on the sensations in your feet.
- For the next breath, shift your focus to the physical sensations in your lower legs.
- Gradually move your awareness up your body with each breath: upper legs, hips and pelvis, lower torso, upper torso, upper arms, lower arms, shoulders, neck, head. Spend one full breath cycle (in and out) on each body part.

- It's natural for your mind to drift to other thoughts. When you notice this, gently and kindly bring your focus back to your body, continuing from where you left off.
- Conclude by spending a few breaths experiencing your body as a whole. Try to cultivate a sense of affection for your body if possible. If not, that's perfectly fine – just do your best and see what unfolds.

Increasing Sensory Awareness: (Suggested for morning)

- Find a calm and comfortable place where you can sit or lie down easily.
- Take some big breaths to calm down and focus on the now.
- Start by paying attention to each of your five senses, one by one. Check out the feelings and things you notice with each sense.
- **Sight**: Open your eyes and look around. See the colors, shapes, and designs around you. Look at any things or details that grab your eye. Take some time to just enjoy the look of your place.
- **Hearing**: Move your focus to the sounds you hear. Listen to the quiet noises around you. Hear any far-off sounds, and those close to you. Listen to the beat, high or low sound, and type of the sounds. Take a moment to enjoy the mix of sounds around you.
- **Smell**: Pay attention to your sense of smell. Breathe in deep and smell any smells in the air. Whether it's the smell of flowers, fresh coffee, or nature, let yourself fully feel and enjoy the different smells you notice.
- **Taste**: Move your focus to your sense of taste. If you can, take a sip of a drink or a bite of a snack. Pay close attention

to the tastes, how it feels, and feelings in your mouth. Notice the different tastes as you chew or swallow. Let yourself fully enjoy each bite or sip.

- **Touch**: Lastly, pay attention to what you can touch. Feel how your body feels against what you're sitting or lying on. Feel the air's temperature on your skin. Run your hands over different things nearby and feel what they feel like. Check out the different things you can feel.
- After checking out each sense one by one, take a moment to bring all your senses together. Notice how they work together to make your overall feeling of the now.
- Take a few more big breaths and slowly bring your focus back to where you are. Think about the experience and how it has changed how you feel and your overall health.

<u>Object contemplation:</u>

- Pick an object that's easy to hold in your hand. Hold it in one hand and then the other. Feel how heavy or light it is. How big is it? Run your fingers over it. Are the edges rough or smooth? Look at the shape, color, and feel of the object. Feel any bumps or dips. Notice if it feels smooth or rough. Does it feel cold or warm? Is it sticky, oily, slippery, wet, or dry?
- Look closely to see if there's anything written on it. Are there words or pictures on it? If your mind starts to wander or you start to feel bored, just bring your focus back to the object. Squeeze it. Is it soft, bendy, hard, or firm?
- What sound does it make when you tap on it with your finger or scratch it with your nail? Does it echo, thud, click, thump, rattle? Turn it in your hand. How does the light bounce off it? Is it shiny or dull? Does it reflect light like a

mirror? Is the color solid, cloudy, see-through? Can you see through it? Is it solid or empty? What's it made of?

- Hold it up to your nose and smell it. Does it smell? Is it stinky, sweet, or no smell? Can you drop it on the table? Does it stay still or roll around or wobble? What sound does it make as you move it on the table? Does it slide easily or stick? Look closely and find something you didn't see before.

<u>Walking Meditation:</u>

Environment-Centric walk:

Initiate your walk with the goal of being mindful of your environment. If you're outdoors, start by observing the ground you're walking on and the sensation in your feet as they move. Then, broaden your observation. Take note of the weather, the temperature, the wind, the sky, and the clouds. Observe the trees, their leaves, bark, and branches. Concentrate on flowers, grass, fields, lakes, or streams. Spot animals like squirrels, dogs, cats, and birds. Tune into the sounds. Detect any scents or smells you encounter. If you're in a city, look for natural beauty in places like sidewalk trees, flower pots, gardens, and parks. Also, pay attention to the buildings, streets, businesses, vehicles, and people. Observe the colors, sounds, and energy in your vicinity. If you find your thoughts drifting away from your surroundings, gently redirect your focus to what you can visually perceive. Continue this until your walk ends.

Reflective Walk:

Pick a topic or problem that is closely linked to your own identity and who you would be without this story. Make it your focal point. Start your walk, keeping your chosen subject in mind. Each time you find your thoughts straying, acknowledge it and refocus on your chosen subject. Stay alert to your surroundings for safety. Let your steps serve as a reminder to maintain your focus as you intended. Continue this until your walk concludes.

Informal

Informal meditation, also known as daily life meditation, is the practice of integrating mindfulness into your routine tasks. Rather than designating a particular time and location for meditation, you seek moments throughout your day to be completely present and conscious. This could be while doing activities like walking, taking a shower, doing the dishes, or even while conversing. The goal is to remain mindful and alert, concentrating on the pure perception of the experience without any mental commentary. It's about transforming regular activities into chances for total presence. The more you engage in formal meditation, the simpler it becomes to weave informal meditation into your everyday life.

Outside:

Give this a try whenever you're outdoors, be it during a walk, while sitting outside, or en route to your car. Make an effort to remain present and observe your surroundings when you're outside.

Begin with the sky. Observe its color. Is it cloudless or cloudy? How do the clouds appear? Can you see the sun? Is it obscured by clouds? Is it daytime or nighttime?

Next, look around. Do you see any trees? If so, examine one tree in detail. Are there leaves on it or are the branches bare?

What color are the leaves or branches? Can you spot any buds, seeds, or flowers on the branches? Does it have pine needles and cones? Is the tree stationary or swaying in the wind?

Take a slow, deep breath and identify any smells. Can you detect a scent? Is it pleasant or unpleasant? Does it originate from nature or is it artificial? Does it evoke any memories or remind you of a particular time in your life?

Do you see grass? What's its color? Is it lush and green or dry and brittle? Is it tall or short? If possible, touch the grass. How does it feel?

Are there flowers? Observe their colors and shapes. Smell them if you can.

Do you see any rocks? Examine their shape and color. Touch them and notice their texture.

Can you see a lake or the ocean? Observe the water. Is it tranquil and still or rippling with waves? What's the color of the water? Is there a beach?

Listen carefully. What sounds can you hear? Are birds chirping? Can you hear urban noises like cars, trucks, planes, engines, horns, sirens? Can you hear the rustling of the wind in the trees? Is there a sound from a stream, waterfall, or ocean waves?

Feel the temperature on your skin. Is it hot, cold, warm, or cool? Is the air still or is there a breeze?

After spending some time truly observing the nature around you, carry this heightened awareness with you as you resume your day.

Inside:

Tea/Coffee Making: Pay attention to each step of the process - the sound of the water boiling, the smell of the tea or coffee, the warmth of the cup in your hands.

Ironing: Notice the sensation of the iron moving over the clothes, the sound of the steam, and the transformation of the wrinkled fabric into smooth.

Vacuuming: Focus on the sensation of movement, the sound of the vacuum, and the immediate result of a cleaner surface.

Plant Care: If you have houseplants, spend time tending to them. Notice the color and health of the leaves, the feel of the pot, and the smell of the earth.

Reading: Choose a book and read it slowly. Absorb the words, visualize the story, and tune into the emotions it brings up.

Art: Engage in drawing, painting, or any other art activity. Observe the colors, the movement of your hands, and the emerging creation.

Knitting/Sewing: If you knit or sew, focus on the pattern, the feel of the material, and the rhythm of your movements.

Dishwashing: Pay attention to the sensation of the water and soap on your hands, the sound of the water, and the sight of the bubbles.

Cooking: Notice the colors and smells of the ingredients, the sound of the chopping, and the heat from the stove.

Cleaning: Be it sweeping, dusting, or organizing, focus on the task at hand. Notice the movements of your hands and the feeling of the objects.

Laundry: Observe the process of sorting, washing, and folding. Feel the texture of the clothes and listen to the sound of the washing machine.

Eating: Eat slowly, savoring each bite. Pay attention to the taste, texture, and smell of the food.

Showering: Notice the sensation of the water on your skin, the sound of the water, and the smell of the soap or shampoo. The raw experience of the temperature of water.

Gardening: If you have indoor plants, take time to water them, prune them, or simply observe their growth. Notice the color and texture of the leaves, the moisture of the soil, and the smell of the plants.

Notes and Insights

Notes and Insights

www.ingramcontent.com/pod-product-compliance
Lightning Source LLC
LaVergne TN
LVHW091059150826
845673LV00002B/641

* 9 7 9 8 8 9 2 7 7 1 9 7 9 *